IT'S TIME TO

Believe in Yourself

The Pathway Home

TAMMY OBRIEN

 FriesenPress

One Printers Way
Altona, MB R0G 0B0
Canada

www.friesenpress.com

ISBN
978-1-03-918825-9 (Hardcover)
978-1-03-918824-2 (Paperback)
978-1-03-918826-6 (eBook)

1. BODY, MIND & SPIRIT, SPIRITUALISM

Distributed to the trade by The Ingram Book Company

Spiritual Devotional

We are all in this together.

We are all one.

We are all connected.

We are all life.

We are all love.

We are all God.

Written by T. O'Brien

About My Artwork

This book contains twelve pieces of my artwork that
I have been inspired to paint over the years.

This artistic gift of mine is one that I love very much.

I enjoy **painting** scenery, flowers, butterflies, birds, animals,
and houses. I truly love to paint anything and everything.

I also do commissioned artwork for others,
bringing their photographs to life.

I specialize in pet portraits and house art, and
these are my favourites pieces to paint.

Painting, writing, and helping others to change
their lives are truly passions of mine.

You can find all of my favourite artwork compiled on
my website, and I am always adding more.

There are prints available, some originals,
commission work, as well as merchandise.

www.tammysfineartandcommissions.ca

Please check out the site and order your favourites or contact
me if you would like any commissioned work done.

All of the pieces in this book are available for prints,
and your support is greatly appreciated.

I own the rights to all the artwork, and no reproductions are allowed.

I hope you enjoy the art and the healing words in this book.

These devotions are timeless, and they can
help you at any time in your life.

Dedication

This book is dedicated to my Facebook group "It's Time to Believe in Yourself," of which I am the administrator and spiritual mentor, facilitating the words that are posted daily.

I was inspired by a higher power to create this group in October 2021, and this higher power then guided me with wisdom and knowledge to share healing words with others as I awakened on the path of enlightenment.

I will refer to this higher power as God, source energy, my higher self, and my soul.

This group has helped me to believe in myself, and it has also helped my members to find healing, become better people, see a new way of living and being, and align with their true self.

I posted these spiritual lessons, teachings, and uplifting messages almost daily for everyone to see.

As I write this, there are currently 45,000 members in the "It's Time to Believe in Yourself" group, and each of us is being divinely guided to help heal and change people at this time of awakening into a new era.

A golden era.

My goal with this group is to assist people to raise their vibration so that we can shift into this higher dimension that we are moving toward.

Foreword

This book is divinely led.

I have been inspired to compile my words of healing into a one-year devotional so that they can be easily accessed on a daily basis.

These timeless words are for everyone, and they will help you anytime and anywhere.

This book may trigger you, but that's good, because it means you're healing.

The words within these pages can help you change your life for the better, step by step, day by day, and by living in the moment every day.

Loving your life and loving yourself are priorities, and with each individual that heals and changes their vibration and energy to the positive, it's helping to awaken the earth to a place of peace and love and harmony.

It's Time to Believe in Yourself is a guidebook on your path to healing and to living your true path and life.

To use this book, start with day one, as it doesn't matter when you begin, day one is the beginning of your healing journey.

Read the message and reflect on it to heal, to uplift you, to help you go within, and to change your perspective in your day.

Journal at the end of your day, reflecting on the message and the good things that happened to you in your day, and taking a moment to appreciate what you already have in your life.

Thank God and your spirit guides for helping you throughout your day, asking for their guidance when you awaken and expressing gratitude to them before you sleep.

They are always with you.

Another way to use this book is to randomly open it to a page and read that devotion.

This is your message to reflect on for the day.

Always stay positive and lead your life with your heart, and love yourself and God unconditionally.

Put yourself and your own well-being first.

You cannot pour from an empty cup, so you have to give to yourself first, then you can help and inspire others on the way.

This is the start of your healing journey and becoming the best version of you as you move forward, one day at time and in the moment.

Always Believe in Yourself.

T. OBrien

A New Beginning

This is my favourite piece of artwork.

It was the first painting that I made when I started my healing path.

My life was starting over again, and I was beginning a journey
to my true self, although I did not know that at the time.

I was afraid and alone, but after painting this I felt new. I was on a
path to a better life, and it felt so good to know this in my heart.

Day 1

Mental health is so important in your life.

Your mind runs your entire life.

What you see, hear, taste, feel, touch, and smell is all from your mind.

Your job, family, passions, emotions, body, and anything
you do and say are all coming from your mind.

Yet you neglect and abuse it.

And you don't even try to fix it.

Because you can't see your mind.

It's so used to those negative vibrations running the show.

What are you doing today to change your mental health?

Ignoring it? Suffering with it? Hurting from it?

Or are you loving your mind, using it to create
an amazing life, path, family, and you?

Your mindset and well-being are so important to
keep healthy so you can live a great life.

This book will guide you to a new perspective and a new way of living.

You need to be a positive, loving, kind, compassionate
being, as this is who you truly are.

When you have a healthy, positive mindset, you
can create a beautiful and abundant life.

Start changing your life today.

Day 2

You have to begin to view the world from a different perspective.

Your thoughts create your reality on your path.

Your mindset is everything along the way.

You need to change to a new outlook, starting today.

The old ways are not working, and they are keeping you stuck.

A negative mind creates a negative life.

What's the energy of the path that you are on?

Negative or positive?

Start to look at the positive in every situation and in
every person that you meet on your journey.

Begin to see all the beautiful nature, people, and animals that
are created by God on this earth for you to admire and love.

This small act of practicing positivity will
change your life tremendously.

Make this your goal for the new year, to create
a fresh, beautiful path and a new you.

Day 3

Life will only get better if you choose it.

The choice is yours and only yours.

Deciding to be better comes when you can surrender to yourself.

When you can choose you over a toxic
behaviour, substance, or emotions.

When you choose love over fear, you will begin to change.

When you choose you over a toxic relationship
or person, you will start to heal.

When you put yourself first, you will start to change.

To choose love is to heal your heart.

To choose fear is to shrink your heart into your ego.

Life will only get better when you choose to
step into your own love for you.

Day 4

Healing is hard; no one ever said it was easy.

You have to face the hard part of your life in order to change.

Healing means changing who you have become into
someone that is better and to who you are meant to be.

You have to believe that what you are healing from will help
you to change and grow into this beautiful, new person.

You have to see who you are not before you
can become who you truly are.

The people you are healing from are showing you what you
need to learn and do in order to make this transformation.

It's hard because you can't see past the now of what is.

You are transforming and transitioning into your true self.

Don't be afraid; it's all part of the divine plan of your soul and of God.

They are showing you the way to who they
know you can become again.

Your spirits and God believe in you and have faith in you,
and they love you so much that they support you and guide
you to the path you need to take on this healing journey.

You cannot continue to be the same anymore.

You cannot continue to hurt anymore.

You deserve happiness, love, and joy; everyone does.

You are a pure, positive soul, and you are finding your
way back to our true self and back home to God.

Your soul and God have been waiting for this moment of healing,
growth, and evolution for many, many, many lifetimes.

4 — Tammy O'Brien

You are finally here.

You are on the journey home to healing and alignment with your true self.

Don't be afraid to change and step onto this path.

It's a beautiful, transformational process.

Keep healing; you are almost there.

You will be in alignment with God.

God is leading you back home.

Back to heaven on earth.

Back to pure, positive energy and unconditional love for yourself, for your path, for God, and your soul.

Day 5

Have faith in yourself.

Faith is knowing that you will survive anything.

Faith is knowing that everything will work
out the way it is supposed to.

Faith is knowing that God has your back and
that you can always lean on him.

Faith is knowing that God's love and light are shining on you always.

Faith is surrendering to that love and light of God.

Faith is letting God lead you today and every day.

This is true faith in yourself and God.

Give your trust and faith to God, as He is your partner for eternity.

Have faith in yourself, and it will change your
life into the love of God on your path.

$\mathcal{D}ay$ **6**

Failure is only in your eyes.

Only you are seeing it.

Failure is growth and failure is only how you perceive it.

No one is a failure in life.

No one.

You're not a failure.

You are living life.

Stop trying to please everyone else on your path.

Start doing things for you.

Just be.

Live in the moment, and just be who you are.

There is no work here, only creating a life
that you love, not a life for others.

You may feel like a failure when you let other people
down by not living up to their expectations.

But you are never a failure.

Never.

You are succeeding everywhere you go.

Keep moving forward and into more love for your life.

Be proud of your journey.

Be proud of who you are.

Day 7

Stop looking back at your life so much.

You have already created that.

That's the old life and the old you.

You are not that person anymore or ever again.

You cannot ever be that person again.

You evolved, you grew, and you learned from
the people and the experiences.

Only look back if it will make you stronger, more
aware, and if it will raise your consciousness.

Only look back to see the amazing parts of you, then
bring them forward into the present moment.

There is no dwelling, no more hurting or pain to keep holding on to.

It was there to help you create a new and
better you and a better future.

Move forward, not backwards.

The past cannot steer your life because it's behind you now.

Put yourself in the driver's seat so you can control your own life again.

Day 8

If you really want to change your life, do it.

Move forward into change and into a new direction because you truly want to be a better person and have a happier life.

Do it positively.

Do it with happy emotions.

Do it with bravery.

Do it because you want to.

Do it to feel better.

Have goals and motivation to become a better version of yourself.

In the process, don't put yourself down or blame others for your decisions, as this only hinders you and sets you back.

Do it because you love yourself and because you want more of that in your life.

When you start focussing on you and your new path and the good, your whole world will shift and become amazing.

Appreciate everything, especially you and your life, and you will be unstoppable.

Day 9

Your mindset is so powerful.

It's the most powerful tool you have to create your lives.

Did you know that you create your own life and path?

Does your life in this present moment feel good or bad to you?

Do you love your life or hate it?

What kind of mindset do you have?

Positive or negative?

What is in your reality, things you love or hate?

That's an indicator of your mindset.

If your energy is positive and you have a positive mindset, you will attract more and more of the things you want into your life and path.

If your energy is negative and you have a negative mindset, you will attract more and more things you do not want in your life and path.

This is how powerful a tool your mind is.

So, what is it going to take to get you to change your mindset, your vibration, and your energy?

You should want to be happy and have a great life.

Start changing your life today.

Day 10

Forgiving others and yourself is one of the
most important steps of healing.

Forgiveness is the key to healing.

Forgiving yourself changes the way you perceive a situation
and or a person involved on your path and in your life.

Healing involves letting go of old hurts from the past.

Letting go helps you to be present in the now.

If you keep dwelling and reflecting back, you won't move forward.

You will continue to hurt and be stuck on your path.

Forgiving yourself is important.

You are worthy of forgiveness.

You are worthy of being happy.

You are worthy of changing your life for the better.

Let it go so that you can heal, then move on and move forward.

Day 11

Focussing on our passions is what makes us truly happy.

What we want in our life comes when we are truly happy inside.

False happiness is in material things.

They make us temporarily happy in that moment.

It doesn't last.

True happiness is found in our passion for creating our life.

Focussing on what we want isn't always material.

Focussing on peace, love, happiness, bliss, and joy
gives us more of these things in our life.

This is where true happiness is.

We can manifest anything that we focus on when we are
truly aligned and connected with our higher self.

No resistance lives in true happiness and
unconditional love for ourself and our path.

Day 12

God is an important part of our life and path, and we
need to know the truth of who God is in our life.

Knowing this will change our life and how we live it.

God is the creator of all.

God is an energy that is in everything here in this universe.

God is not separate from us.

God is in all of us, and he is in every animal, insect,
plant, cloud, sun, everything, even material things.

We are all energy, the same as God's energy.

God made us from his own energy, and we
are extensions of God, the creator.

Therefore, we are extensions of God.

God is the creator, and we are creators of our life, creating
even more for God, for him to experience through us all.

God experiences life through us, his children, his creations.

We are all one.

We are all created equally in God's eyes.

The energy of God is unconditional love.

Therefore, we are unconditionally loved by God.

Therefore, we are made of this energy of unconditional love as well.

Because we are a part of God's love, we are one with him.

God flows through us.

God lives and creates through us.

God loves us all unconditionally.

We can feel that love if we keep the love flowing
to God always, just as God does to us.

God gives us all we want because of the love flowing through us.

It never stops.

We can create our path together.

If we look away from that love of God with any negative emotions,
we block that flow of love that God is always flowing to us.

God's love never wavers.

Only we waver.

Staying in alignment with unconditional
love keeps the flow moving to us.

God is not a religion, or a person, place, or thing.

God is an energy that is always there, in everyone and in everything.

God is spirit.

God is all things.

God is the creator, and we are God's creators, showing
him our creations so he can experience everything.

God loves everything.

There is no good or bad in God's energy, only creating experiences.

We are all God's children; we are all sons and daughters of God.

We are all eternal, and our energy and our soul never die
because energy never ends, therefore, we never end.

We are energy.

We only transition and transform into different
experiences and realms in the universe.

We are on a journey, and we share it together, with everyone
and with everything, because we are all of this same energy.

The energy of God's unconditional love.

This is the truth of who God is, why we are here, and why we are created.

God is us, and we are God.

Day 13

Alignment is an important part of healing, moving forward, and keeping in a state of joy and happiness, peace, and unconditional love.

To stay in alignment, you need to feel happy, full of love and joy, and be at peace with your life in the moment.

To be in alignment with yourself and life, happiness is the key.

If you want your life to change and to be easy and to go with the flow of life, you need to be in alignment.

To get into alignment, you need to focus on raising your vibration and energy to a state of happiness, joy, bliss, and peace.

To do this, you need to be choosing yourself first.

Doing things you enjoy and focussing on love and blessings that you have in your life, not the lack of them.

Meditation, your passions and purposes, giving and receiving love, and doing the things you love get you into alignment with yourself, your life, and your path.

Alignment has no resistance.

Alignment feels good.

Alignment is the key to getting what you want in life.

Choose alignment and see your life change, grow, expand, and evolve.

More of what you are wanting will come through your path.

Are you in alignment with yourself?

Day 14

An important part of healing and growing and being who
you truly are is being aware of your ego and letting it go.

The ego thinks it knows you.

It doesn't.

It's useless.

It has some uses, but people let the ego control them,
and they live from this space and mindset.

Your ego wants you to be afraid, selfish, rude, angry, resentful, ignorant,
competitive, powerful, and goal-driven for success, fame, and fortune.

It keeps you going down the wrong paths,
continuing to go in circles and to dead ends.

Your ego thinks it knows your wants, and it
wants you to be above everyone.

It sets you up for failure, so then you feel bad, sad, down,
upset, frustrated, depressed, angry, and so forth.

Then you project these things on other people because you are
now blaming them for what happened to you in your life.

But it's because you listened to your ego
instead of your heart and intuition.

Your ego wants things now and done now.

It has no patience and thinks that material things or
other people are going to make you feel better.

Your ego lives in a lack-based world.

In an illusion, a false reality.

It needs possessions, trophies, to win, to have
money, and to be the centre of attention.

But none of these are true self qualities.

They are all false qualities that your ego
drives you into thinking you want.

Your true self, the authentic you that you are
made of, is the total opposite of this.

Your true self is pure, positive energy, unconditional
love, peace, happiness, joy, bliss, calm, creative,
passionate, and at one with God's energy.

Your ego makes you feel separate from all that you truly are.

Your intuition and your heart guide you to all of
the true qualities of your authentic self.

Your ego only guides you away from all that you are.

Drop the egoic mindset and see yourself change, and your
path will flourish, and your life will become beautiful.

You will be on your way to becoming an amazing new person.

Day 15

Affirm this:

Today I appreciate my life.

I appreciate my path.

I appreciate the people who love me.

I appreciate my friends and my family.

I appreciate my love for life.

I am going to appreciate everything that I
receive, looking at them as gifts.

Good or bad, they are things to learn from.

They are showing me something.

I appreciate this new intense feeling of love for my life.

Life is wonderful, and I need to embrace it every day

Day 16

There is always a moment in time when you know you are spiralling downward, and you can probably see the choices you have made that have led you to this point.

You may feel like you are not a good person or worthy enough.

You are good enough and worthy enough.

You are enough.

You are amazing.

You are beautiful.

We are all innately made to be worthy, confident, loving, and good.

It is all in us.

Look at the new that is in this situation in front of you.

It is showing you a lesson so you can move forward.

Be proud and love yourself unconditionally.

Believe in yourself.

Don't be so hard on yourself.

You are doing your best in every moment.

Day 17

The universe offers us gifts every day.

We all receive gifts of abundance, everywhere we look.

When we receive compliments, money, or material
items, these are all gifts from the universe.

These are gifts meant for us, and they are a
part of our abundance and desires.

We need to take them and appreciate them and
thank God for the gifts we receive.

This lets the other person feel good and like they are helping us.

They are now receiving as well.

We need to receive as much as we need to give.

If we don't let ourself receive, we will make it difficult for the
universe to give us what we want and what we are worthy of.

When we stop receiving, we are blocking the universe.

The big things we want in life start with the small things,
and if the universe can't give us the small things, we will
never be able to manifest the bigger things we desire.

Hence, enjoy the little things, as they lead to the bigger things.

$\mathcal{Day}$ 18

Every day choose yourself.

Every day be good to yourself.

Every day do what you love.

Every day show yourself that you love yourself.

Every day show up and be the best you can be.

Every day love your life because no one else will.

Unconditionally love who you are.

Day 19

Start your day in alignment with the love of God.

God's love is unconditional.

God's love is always there, flowing freely and powerfully to all that align with that love.

Today and every day live in the love of God.

Align with it.

Feel it.

Embrace it.

Surrender to God.

Allow God to lead you to where you need to go, inspire you, help you, and support you.

Make God your partner in life.

Go on a journey together and create an amazing and beautiful life in alignment with love.

Day 20

Let go of people, places, and things that no
longer serve your greater good.

Let go of toxic people who make you feel bad, step over your
boundaries, manipulate you, or project their problems on to you.

These people need to go, or you at least need to step back from them.

Your job or places you hang out that are causing negative emotions
and situations that you can't change need to go from your life.

They need to be re-evaluated or readjusted.

That's a sign that you need to change and
leave them for more aligned places.

Letting go of things that are not aligned with your life
path helps you to truly change for the better.

You need to change the things around you that you can.

These things are not resonating with the truth of who you truly are.

Letting go of life as you know it, and changing it
into something new, is truly a beautiful path.

Day 21

We really must work on ourself before we can give to others.

If we are toxic people, we will be spreading toxicity everywhere we go.

To our family, our friends, our co-workers, and the world.

We need to be aware of what we are sending out to others.

We may think we are sending out love because we may be living subconsciously, when really it is going to the other person as negativity, gas lighting, or manipulation.

When we start to love ourself first, showing happiness, self-worth, respect, and unconditional love, the toxicity changes to love and beauty, positivity, happiness, joy, support, helping, good intentions, and peace.

When we are full of love for ourself, we will spread more love to our family, friends, and the world.

This is why it's so important to have self-love and self-care.

Thinking inwardly and forgiving ourself will affect everyone in our life.

Healing ourself helps to heal them as well.

Day 22

You have to start to talk to yourself better.

Never put yourself down.

Look at yourself in the mirror and tell yourself that you are strong, confident, amazing, and beautiful.

If you tell yourself these things, you will start looking at yourself differently.

You will begin to see it and feel it.

Don't ever think you are not worthy.

You were born worthy.

All of us are worthy.

Start to believe in you because you are the only person who counts in your life and on your path.

Day 23

So, you don't believe in the universe, or God, or yourself anymore?

These are all one.

They are all the same and connected.

Faith isn't something you try.

It's something you know.

It's something you trust in.

Believe in yourself and stop trying so hard.

Start listening to your inner voice, your soul.

It is always guiding you, whether you believe or not.

It's there.

You are just so far away from that unconditional
love that you have inside of you.

It's all around you to hear, see, feel, and to know.

It's all around you, calling you to what you want in your life.

The universe, God, and your soul are all here for you every
day, waiting for you to align with them so that you can
believe again and have faith on your path and in yourself.

Day 24

Who you are defines you.

You are unique in every way.

You are on your own unique path in life, and your purpose and gifts are all exclusive to you.

Stop looking to others to define you.

Wishing to be like them.

It's a waste of time, energy, and focus.

You're not seeing your own uniqueness.

You are seeing theirs.

Focus on your path, your life, your gifts, your talents, and your own purpose.

Stay in your own lane.

It's taking you somewhere unique and extraordinary.

So be unique and extraordinary.

Be you.

Day 25

Love is your true self.

Love is the way to a better life and to the truth.

You can stop judging when you live in unconditional love.

Your true self.

That is where we are all going and where we are meant to be.

There is no judgement living in unconditional love
because we have accepted everyone for who they are.

It will stop when we learn that judgement is
an ego-based reality and an illusion.

Everyone seems to judge people at first glance
or at the first sentence they speak.

Don't judge a person.

Judgement is a false belief of another.

It's untrue.

Learn the truth, then stop and accept everyone
for who they are, wherever they are at.

It is not our business to judge anyone for anything
because we have all been there before.

It's our responsibility to change, not the other person.

We need to stop putting people down who we don't even know.

Judgement is the worst kind of negativity.

Judgement shows that we need to heal because
it is reflecting back to us on our path.

It is our responsibility to stop our toxic behaviour, and no one else's.

Love everyone for who they are.

Love is the way to the truth of life.

Not judgement.

That is an egoic mindset.

Love is the way to being a better person and living a better life.

Day 26

When you focus on the good in your life, you'll get more good.

When you focus on the bad in your life, you'll get more bad.

Focussing on the things that are working out in your life
takes the focus off the things that are not working out.

When you release the resistance, you let what you
want into your life when you're not expecting it.

No resistance lets life flow to you.

Day 27

Stop saying the words can't, doesn't, won't, and trying.

Start saying things softer and easier.

"I am finding new ways of looking and new awareness in my mind."

"I am seeing the good in the situation and
letting go of the worry and fear."

"I am moving forward into a new peace and ease in
my mind, and I will feel calm instead of fear."

"I can change my mind, and I can change my life."

Don't those things sound better than saying,
"Nothing works," "I try," or "I can't do it?"

When you change your words, you make your vibration and energy
softer, easier, and calmer instead of the harder can't and won't.

Day 28

Affirm this:

I am ready to speed up my life and level up in my life.

I am asking the universe to move my life forward.

Call me to wherever I need to go on my journey.

I love my journey.

I am always excited to see, feel, touch, know,
and hear the next thing on my path.

I am aware, I am watching, and I am waiting patiently
for my life to move forward to the next exciting person,
place, thing, anything fun, joyful, and that feels good.

Thank you, universe, for all that you bring me.

You surprise and delight me all the time, and I am eager for more.

Day 29

Let life take you where you want to go.

Follow the flow that is on your path.

Let go of the oars and flow where the water takes you.

It may be slow at first, but it will pick up momentum
as you choose to go with the flow of life.

Life will be thrilling and fun as you stop the
resistance and keep moving forward.

Ease and flow.

Let life come to you.

Day 30

If you are worried about something, let it go.

If your mindset is in worry, it is hindering the
good stuff that is coming to you in life.

Worry creates fears, which more than likely are not true.

If you live in this mindset of worry, you are not moving forward in life.

If you are living in the moment, then you are trusting and having
faith that you can handle whatever comes to you in life.

You will make the right choices when they arise.

Worry stops the fun and enjoyment in life.

You are fearing the unknown.

In reality everything moving forward is the
unknown because the future is now.

Have faith that the unknown will come to you and your
life will progress and unfold as it supposed to.

Start living your life again without worry or fear.

Day 31

Love yourself first always.

To start loving yourself, you must start talking to yourself positively.

No putting yourself down.

Start doing the things you love to do every day.

Your passions, your talents, and your gifts are a good place to start.

Start connecting with your higher self.

Meditate and get outside every day.

Start letting go of things that are hurting you.

Let go of anger, resentment, grudges, and hatred.

Start forgiving people because it is only hurting you, not them.

Let it all go.

Forgive yourself.

That's the most important thing in loving yourself.

Everyone has made choices that they thought
were good at the time they made them.

You can't judge the past because it's who you were back
then, and now it's time to change, grow, and evolve.

Forgiveness is an important part in healing yourself.

Loving who you are and not caring what anyone else thinks
about you is something you have to start to do.

Be genuine, be authentic, and be true.

Once you start doing this every day, you will start to feel lighter, freer, and happier, and you will love more because you will feel love in your heart more than ever.

Love yourself.

You are beautiful.

Winter Reflections

This painting draws you into it.

It's so bright and cheery and allows you to
feel warmth on this cold winter day.

The sun lights the snow and brings a feeling of
quietness, peacefulness, and stillness.

Even though it is cold, it's still warm, and the river is calm and gentle.

It's Time to Believe in Yourself — 39

Day 32

Fear is ego.

Fear is anxiety.

Fear is negative emotions.

Fear is unnatural.

Fear is not what your soul or God ever feels.

You are not in alignment with God when you feel fear.

Fear comes from your ego only.

Love is your natural state, not fear.

When you are in fear, you are turning your
thoughts away from the alignment of God.

God is giving you unconditional love always.

When you match that love in your heart, your fear has to leave.

You can't live in fear and in love at the same time.

It's impossible.

Living in love lets the fear go out and the unconditional love come in.

Start matching your soul's love by loving yourself and your life.

Day 33

Everyone is the energy of God, and we are all
one and connected to that energy.

There is only one God.

We are all loved, equally with the energy of God within us.

We are all going back to that same energy when our bodies die.

We all go back to God in heaven; there is no
hell, only love and God's energy.

There is no punishment in the energy of love.

Only lessons, learning, and experiences.

We're all created of love, and our bodies are tools to carry
our souls so that we can experience life here on earth.

We all go to heaven because the energy of God
doesn't judge, shame, hate, or disown any soul.

God's energy is pure love, and it is unconditional.

And that is who we are as well.

We are eternally in this energy.

Therefore, we go to the energy of God in the end.

No one is separate from this energy in this universe, good or
evil, and we all go to heaven to the God we all have within us.

Day 34

Believe in yourself.

Don't wait for others to believe in you.

You have to do this.

You can do this.

You've got this.

You are amazing.

You are beautiful.

You are awesome.

Make today about you and how you feel about you.

Believe in yourself today.

Day 35

Change is always hard at first.

That's why it is called change.

We are changing into new people who we don't even know.

We are moving into the unknown territory of our heart and mind.

Change is hard, but it gets easier and easier
as we practice it more every day.

We can't just stop because something becomes difficult.

There's a lesson that we need to learn on
the other side of the challenge.

There are new paths, new people, and new
adventures waiting for us at the other end.

We can't give up.

We must take one step at a time, and keep going and
flowing through to the next path in our life.

It's there, just waiting for us to embrace it.

$\mathcal{Day}$ 36

When you stop and quiet your mind and listen to your soul
speaking to you, it will take you to amazing places.

It will take you to everything you are desiring.

Your soul knows everything you want and
is taking you there on your path.

Listen to your soul and enjoy the journey it takes you on.

Surrender to your soul.

It's truly amazing.

Day 37

Live in the moment.

Live in the now.

There is no suffering in the now.

Just what you choose to experience.

Suffering is a choice from not living in the now.

Only love is in the now.

Feel the love for you in the here, the now, and in this moment.

Day 38

Affirm this:

Thank you spirit guides for all that you do
for me every minute of my day.

I know you are with me, loving me, guiding me,
showing me, leading me, and believing in me.

I see it, feel it, know it, believe it, love it, and appreciate it.

I give you my full attention, moving forward into
new paths and adventures that we are on.

I am excited, eager, and ready for what comes on my path.

I surrender all of my resistance, negativity, and toxic energy to you,
my spirit guides, for you to transmute into something beautiful.

We are in this together, so let's change my life, other
people's lives, and show them what we are made of.

Let's change together.

I am ready.

Day 39

Everyone's self-worth is equal in the world.

Your worth isn't about what you own, what you look like, what job you have, or how much money you make.

It's not material.

It's about loving who you are unconditionally and having compassion and empathy for yourself and your path.

It's about believing in yourself, standing up for yourself, and being true to yourself.

It's about living for you, not for others.

Your self-esteem, self-respect, and knowing who you are, are so important on your path today.

Your self-worth is really your true and best self.

$\mathcal{D}ay$ 40

Your heart leads you home.

That's where it is leading you.

You are divinely led.

You are beautifully led on your path.

You are guided.

Your heart takes you there.

Back home to God.

Everyone is connected by their heart spaces.

Your heart continuously leads you to the beautiful path laid down by God for you to follow.

Always listen to what your heart says.

It's God's words showing you the way.

If your heart is pulling you forward, then that's the route that's closer to something magnificent.

Lead with your heart.

It's the path home to God.

Day 41

Life is good.

Life is beautiful.

If you keep saying life is unfair, then it will be.

You get what you focus on in life.

Your life will be unfair if that's what you believe
and are focussing on every day.

If you focus on living, choosing to look at the beauty
in yourself, and you are grateful and appreciative for
everything around you, then your life will change.

Love changes everything.

You have to do the work, though.

Life will continue to be unfair if that's what you think every day.

Your thoughts create your reality.

Have you ever tried to think positively instead of negatively?

Being negative won't work for you, if you want to change.

Changing your mindset is a great step to transforming your life.

Your mindset makes or breaks your life.

What you think is what you get.

You are the creator of your own life.

You manifest into your life what you focus on,
what you think, and what you say.

If you keep saying life is unfair, it will be, and it will only get worse.

Think positively because the negative doesn't work anymore.

Think: "My life is great."

"I love everything in my life, including myself, and I have the freedom to do anything I want to."

"I have all that I need right now, right here."

"Thank you, God, for giving me this beautiful life and for all that I am receiving; it's beautiful, and I am grateful for it."

When you change your words, your attitude, and your perspective on your life to good, it changes your path, your life, and what you receive in it.

You attract who you are.

You attract what you think.

You attract everything into your life, good or bad.

We are all powerful creators, and we don't even know it.

If you want your life to improve, then you have to live a different way than you have been.

The old way doesn't work.

Try a new way to get a new life, a new path, and a new you.

Day 42

Affirm this:

I wake up with a smile every day.

I wake up ready to walk my path.

I am alive and excited to be doing the things I love every day.

I am excited to create more of a life I love.

I am ready to see the beauty of my day all around me.

I am ready to feel it in me.

I am here to create a life I love today and every day.

I am proud of all that I have created in my life.

It's mine, and I love it.

My life is beautiful.

I am beautiful.

Today is my day to shine and to spread light wherever I go.

Thank you, God, for giving me my light to shine bright.

 Day 43

Keep feeling the light and love and move
toward what they are telling you.

Anything that feels like love, move in that direction.

Anything that feels bad, don't move in that direction.

It is your ego talking to you.

Let it go.

Tell it to be quiet, then think and feel the opposite.

Feel the warmth of the light and love, that's where the truth of life is.

That's where the love of life is.

Keep doing the things you love every day, and that
will keep you moving forward into more love.

Love is everywhere.

Day 44

Affirm this:

I am truly a person who is full of love and happiness
and is connected to the universe.

I am at ease with my life, and it flows exactly where I want it to go.

Ease and flow are my life, and I love it.

I live in the present moment every day.

I enjoy seeing what the universe brings to me each and every day.

I am eager for what surprises it has for me.

I am an independent, strong, powerful, intuitive, open-
minded, passionate, beautiful, loving, and caring person.

There are no limits to what I can do, or be, or go on my path.

I love my life, my path, and my relationships.

I love who I am becoming.

I love where I am going.

I love the journey.

It's truly amazing.

Keep giving me all that I am wanting.

I am loving and appreciating it all.

My life is amazing.

Thank you for my life.

Day 45

If you want to change your life, you have to start changing
your old ways into new ways of being and thinking.

You have to raise and change your vibration and energy.

You have to change your intentions.

You have to put this new intention at the front of your path.

Your intention to change has to be your focus.

Don't let anyone or anything change your focus back to your old ways.

Don't be manipulated by others with their ill intentions.

Some people won't want you to change because they know that if they
don't change and grow with you, they know they will be left behind.

When you change, you can help others around you change too.

Just be aware of the ones who may not want you to
change, and they will try and drag you back down.

Keep your distance from them if you are focussing on changing.

If they are not supporting you or helping you,
then they are not for you in this moment.

Take time for you to change, to grow, and to become better.

When your intentions are pure, all that you need
from the universe will show up for you.

The tools, the mentors, the teachers, the time,
and the energy will flow to you.

The universe wants you to align with it.

The universe will be supporting you and guiding you.

The universe is always for you, never against you.

Day 46

Let it go.

That's not you anymore, and what you are holding
on to has made you who you are today.

Everyone goes through situations in life that help them move forward.

If you didn't experience bad situations in life, you would be stuck.

Let it go.

You learn something from every situation, and you
can't move forward until you learn the lesson.

Be proud that you are experiencing life and you are growing.

Find the lesson and learn it.

Let it go.

And look forward to a new beginning and a new you.

Day **47**

Action isn't always the best.

Sometimes you need to relax, let things
unfold, and let life come to you.

Trust that things will unfold the way they should.

You will see and feel what you have to do
next, when things start to happen.

Trust and faith.

Not action and force.

Let things flow to you naturally and let the
resistance of forcing things go.

It will change your life when you start to live this way.

Living in the moment every day and letting your life
unfold naturally is the way to live your life.

$\mathcal{D}ay$ **48**

Worry is really a useless trait or emotion.

It does absolutely nothing to help a situation, and it makes us feel like something bad is going to happen all the time.

Which to be truthful, nothing bad ever happens.

We have experiences that need to happen so we can learn, evolve, grow, and change.

Having faith that everything is going to unfold as it should and that everything will be ok, changes how we see our life.

Living in worry is living in fear.

Living in worry is wasting our life.

Living in worry stops us from moving forward and enjoying life.

Living in worry makes us feel stuck.

Living in worry stops us from experiencing new things, new people, and a different life.

We need to stop worrying about things or people in our life.

It hurts us, our life, and our path.

Choosing faith is always the right path.

Day 49

Happiness is living in the moment and letting life come to you.

Not forcing any moment, just letting it happen.

Happiness is saying yes to the things that
feel good and embracing them.

Happiness is letting go of the things that
weigh you down so you can be free.

Happiness is creating your life from a place
of love and peace in your heart.

Happiness is the freedom to choose your
own path and follow your destiny.

Happiness is a choice that comes from inside
your heart, your soul, and your mindset.

Happiness is in each and every one of us.

Look inside your soul, find your happiness, and start living it today.

$\mathcal{D}ay$ 50

Every minute that goes by is gone, and we cannot change it.

We cannot dwell on the mistakes and regrets in our past.

We forget that life is right now.

We forget to live in the now.

We need to start learning from the past so that we can
create a more beautiful life moving forward.

If we appreciate the now, we don't have to worry about what is coming
to us because we will always have more love and blessings flow our way.

Live for the now, not the past or the future.

Day 51

Today and moving forward, let go of the control
of wanting something right away.

Let go of the control of not knowing when, where, what,
who, or how things are going to unfold and come to you.

The universe knows.

It knows everything,

It knows everything you want and desire.

When you let go of the control, you let go of the resistance, and
you let what you want come into your path at the perfect time.

The universe knows you.

The universe will surprise and delight you with everything.

Have faith and trust.

The universe knows everything.

And the universe truly knows you.

Day 52

The healing process and the awakening of your
soul are very similar to each other.

Awakening is an even deeper knowing, though.

It's a knowing of who you are and how the universe works.

It's a way of living and surrendering to the universe and using
your guidance system, God's energy, to lead the way.

You are using your intuition now in awakening instead of your ego.

First, to get to this process of life, you must heal
your past traumas, then let them go.

You need to forgive and learn to let go.

Accept what is and move forward.

You must shed your limited beliefs and open up your
mind to the endless possibilities of the universe.

Embrace faith, trust, live in love, and live in
the moment where life truly resides.

Healing is powerful.

It will change your life and path into something incredible.

Learn to let go, forgive, live in the present, and open your mind to a
new way of being, living, thinking, and surrendering to the universe.

When you heal, you will change your life, the people around you will
be affected, and you can start to help change the world for the better.

When you stop living outside of your egoic
mind, the world will be at peace.

Healing is so important so that you can awaken to who
you truly are and why you are here on this earth.

Day 53

We all have limiting beliefs on our abilities
to be the people we want to be.

We allow society, our family, and our friends
to make us feel less than we are.

But we are all amazing human beings.

Our mind is our superpower.

Use your mind to believe in yourself.

To have confidence, to have determination, and
to move forward into something new.

Start believing in who you are and what you
want to be and do, and it will happen.

It will unfold.

It will manifest in your life.

Push yourself out of your comfort zone.

Do it.

It's amazing.

Make today the day you say yes.

You can do this.

Believe in yourself today.

Day 54

You do not need fixing; you are never broken.

You are wherever you are in this present moment.

You are looking for peace, happiness, and joy.

The only way to find these things is in the present moment.

Drop that past thinking.

Drop that future thinking.

Drop that worry.

Drop that anxiety.

Drop that depression.

These things will disappear when you let life come to you.

When you live in the present moment, you will no longer feel broken.

Day 55

Everything is a learning process that you have to practice every day.

You have to choose to make better choices
and to have a different mindset.

It's a life change.

It's a new way of living and being.

Meditation, walking, focussing on the good and the positive,
changing your words, and journalling your thoughts should
be added to your daily routine to help you to change.

Stop saying negative things, such as: "This is hard,"
"It's easier said than done," and "I can't."

Quiet your mind with meditation every day.

Be aware of your negative thoughts and
change them to something positive.

Stop looking at the bad and start looking at the good.

Changing your mindset is the most important
thing you can do to stop your ego.

Mindset is everything.

Everyone can change and do it.

It's up to you whether you want to put in the effort, time,
willpower, and dedication to changing your life.

Many people struggle with change because they don't put the effort in.

It means doing something new and different.

Change takes time; it doesn't happen overnight.

But it will be worth it for a better life and a better you.

Day 56

Thank you, God, for being in my life and guiding me to my truest, highest self, that is aligned with your love.

I am that love.

We are that love.

Together we will walk through this universe as spiritual beings on a path of healing, love, beauty, and peace.

We will spread this energy to the world.

It will flow from me, and it will flow from you, this magnificent life force energy that everyone will feel from us.

We will help others see the light.

We will help others feel the light.

We will help others feel the love.

We will help others be this energy.

Thank you, God, for being my partner on this journey, and for helping me see, feel, know, and be my truest self again.

Day 57

Hope is the feeling of new thinking, that there are new paths coming to you in every moment, in every person you meet, and in every situation.

Hope is a desire for more.

Hope means life.

Hope means love.

Hope means truth.

Hope means desire.

Hope means more to come.

If you have no hope, you cannot see the new path, the new desires, the new people, or the new situations coming to you.

If you have no hope, then you are blind, and you have lost your way, your direction, and your love for life.

Hope brings peace, love, new thoughts, new ideas, and new life into your path.

So, don't lose hope, or you will end up losing love for your life.

Day 58

I am here in you, for you.

I am here to listen, and I am here to help you through your day.

I am here to guide you, uplift you, and support you.

I am in you to show you the way to self-love, to worthiness,
to forgiveness, to kindness, and to peace.

I am here in you to feel your creation in life, so
you will see it, to know it, and be it.

I am here in you to flow through you, to heal
you, to love you, and to create with you.

I am here in you every moment of every day.

I am God in you.

We are one.

We are walking this life together for eternity.

Day 59

Affirm this:

I am flowing with positive energy today.

My thoughts are high.

My visions of my path are beautiful.

I am focussing on the love and the light in my
path, and I am attracting it all into me.

I am drawing what I want to me with positive energy and vibration.

That energy is flowing without doubts, fears, or anything
negative to block what I want in my life.

Everything I desire is on its way to my path.

I have only love flowing.

My vibration is rising, and so is my life.

I am flowing as I focus on what I want, not on what I don't.

I am attracting my life right now, and everything I want
is flowing to me as I love my life and my path.

Thank you for everything I receive today.

I have attracted it to me with my high-flying vibration and energy.

I am the creator of my own life.

Pure Joy

This is one of my favourite pieces of artwork.

She just oozes joy and happiness and innocence.

She is being her true self.

We all need to feel this joy every day on our path.

This piece of artwork makes me feel so happy when I see it.

It brings a feeling of higher child-like energy that we all need to experience more of in our lives.

$\mathcal{D}ay$ **60**

Relax, inhale, exhale, and breathe.

Feel the calmness around you.

Feel the serenity flowing in the air around you.

Relax, inhale, exhale, and breathe.

Close your eyes to the reality of the day.

Close off the chaos, the stress, and the noise.

Close off those thoughts of doubt, frustration, anger, sadness, and hate.

Close it all off.

Relax, inhale, exhale, and breathe.

Open up your mind to stillness, to appreciation, and to love.

Open up your mind receive inspiration, creation, and manifestation.

Open your mind up to the new, inspired thought
that will take you somewhere amazing.

Hear the messages loud and clear in the stillness.

This is the moment that you are aligned with
the universe and at peace with yourself.

Relax, inhale, exhale, and breathe.

This is peace.

Day 61

You need to remember that you come first, then others.

You cannot give what you don't have.

You have to be responsible for your own well-being,
happiness, choices, life, personal growth, and self.

You need to stop worrying about what other people think.

They are not living or creating your life.

It's not your responsibility to make other people
happy; that is their responsibility.

It isn't your responsibility to take blame from
others; that is their responsibility.

You are the most important person in your life who can make a
difference in your path and in the direction that your life takes you.

You need to remember that the love you give
yourself is the most important thing.

You are responsible for your own happiness,
thoughts, words, vibration, and energy.

Love yourself more every day, and don't look at anyone else's path.

Stay on your own path and own it because it's yours and yours only.

Day 62

We are all made of unconditional love.

We are all perfect, unique, individual souls,
capable of something extraordinary.

We all have passions and talents to help us be extraordinary.

These gifts lead us to our path and purpose.

They are God given.

To think otherwise is to turn away from that light of
unconditional love that is flowing to us and through us.

Always look and feel for the love of the universe
because that's what makes us extraordinary.

Be extraordinary.

Be you.

Day 63

Drop the heavy baggage that you are walking around with today.

It's heavy and only a burden.

Let it go, drop it, and ignore it.

It's not doing you any good or any favours.

Your past doesn't have to go where you go, and
you don't need to tell people about it.

Talk about the good parts of your past if you must, but nothing more.

Stop reliving it.

People want to hear about who you are now, today, in the present.

Because that's the important person right here and now.

Go ahead and drop that heavy weight today.

You will feel so strong when you let go of it.

You will be stronger.

You will have more strength to move forward
without the baggage weighing you down.

Let it go.

You don't need it anymore.

Day 64

Everyone comes to us for a reason.

To teach us something.

We are born in a family to teach us something.

We have a relationship to teach us something.

We have children to teach us something.

We have friends to teach us something.

We have co-workers to teach us something.

Everyone in our life is a teacher to us.

And we are a teacher to them.

As the teacher teaches, the student also learns on the path.

We are all teachers and students on this earth.

What are the people around you teaching you,
and what are you learning from them?

This will deepen your connection, and it will help you
to see the truth and understand the reason behind the
friendship, or whatever relationship the person is to you.

If it is toxic, it will help you find the reason
to leave that connection as well.

You can wake up to it and change from it and make
a different choice, if that is necessary to do.

What are you learning from the souls around you?

They come to show you something about
yourself, your life, and your path.

Day 65

Affirm this:

I have no fear in my life.

I have no fear of making mistakes or doing the wrong thing.

I have no fear because I am doing what I think is right.

I have no fear because I know that failure and challenges in every aspect of my life are how I grow and evolve and get better.

I have no fear of being myself, and I have no fear of my failure because I trust in myself and God.

We are together on this path, which makes me fearless.

Thank you for making me fearless in my life.

I am brave, courageous, and I am the leader of my life.

I am the creator of my life, and I am done fearing anything that comes on my path.

Thank you, God, for being by my side every minute of my day.

Day 66

It takes sixty-six days of consistency to change a
habit, to stop a habit, or break a pattern.

To change your life, you need to be consistent as well.

You need to stay motivated, aware, and inspired to keep going.

Sixty-six days to a new lifestyle or better habits.

It's something you have to work at every day.

But once you get going it becomes part of your day and part of you.

Stay motivated and inspired.

Keep going.

To a better you.

Day 67

Any negative emotions or circumstances that you experience
are a sign from the universe that change is coming.

Change is necessary in your life when this is happening.

When your life is in upheaval, spiralling downward,
intense, or in a state of chaos, it's time to open your
eyes, your mind, and listen to your soul's message.

See and feel the emotion and energy.

Negative energy means change.

When you resist that change and stay the same, the universe
will bring it back to you in a different way for you to see it.

These experiences are here to wake you up and move
you forward into a new path and direction.

They are here to help you grow and learn a lesson in life so
that you can become a better person in the next path.

If you choose to ignore these experiences, they will be
repeated and repeated until you finally learn the lesson.

These are toxic patterns and behaviours that you need to shed.

If you choose to see the gift in these experiences and move forward
into change, then you allow better things to come into your life.

They are preparing you for a new chapter and a better path for you.

The sooner you see it, the sooner you can live your life again
from a better mindset, perspective, and awareness.

Day 68

Stop looking at things you cannot control.

That's what anxiety is.

Stop looking ahead at life.

Live in the now, feeling the now.

There is no life outside of the now.

It's all lies.

You don't know what's going to happen in the next minute even.

Let go of that mindset.

That's what is causing you anxiety.

Control is the problem.

Surrender and trust and have faith that your life will go on as it should.

This is the key to leaving anxiety behind.

Surrender to faith.

You have gotten this far.

And you don't have control; you never do.

You can't control people or situations.

You can only let life come to you and choose in the moment what you want to do with what is showing up for you.

Letting life flow to you without doubts, fears, and worries allows you to live in freedom and in love of your life.

Living in the flow is where life is.

Living in the now, not in the future, not in the past, not in fear of it, and not in doubt of it, is powerful and life changing.

Surrender to the now and love your life.

It will change your life.

Day 69

There is no end to what you can do and to
who you can be on our path.

It's infinite.

There is always more and more.

So don't ever settle.

Don't ever give up.

You are a powerful creators ony our path.

If you focus on the vision of what you want to become, it will come.

You will step closer and closer to it.

The stronger the desire and focus, the more
you will become your true self.

The more you will transform your life into a new person,
a new way of living, and a new way of being.

Sometimes you don't even think it's happening until
you reflect back and see how far you have come.

Don't ever give up on your dreams, goals, or life.

There is always more.

It's unlimited.

You are new every day.

Don't ever think you are not growing, changing,
evolving, and transforming your life every day.

You are.

You have to envision it and feel it.

You have to believe in yourself and become it.

Day 70

You are never alone in this universe.

You have your soul, your spirit guides, God, angels,
and ascended masters all around you.

You have the beauty of the universe around you.

When you start to love yourself and who you are, your heart
will fill with love for life and love for everything around you.

You will never feel alone.

You will not feel sadness in your heart.

You will feel the love of the universe, and you will
feel love, worth, and happiness from within.

Your loneliness is an illusion of the ego because
you are not in a space of love.

You are in a place of sadness.

Happiness comes from the love you have for yourself inside of you.

Not outside of you in people, places, or things.

Start to look for love and goodness and beauty in you.

You will be amazed by how your world and your
feelings will change when you see and feel that love
you have inside of you and surrounding you.

Day 71

If you find something is hard to do, then you have
to look at it from a different perspective.

Many people want to change, grow, and become a better version
of themselves, but then they say, "I want it, but it's too hard."

Have you ever said that about anything?

Probably.

Especially when wanting to heal from something.

It's only hard if you believe it is.

Whatever you think becomes your reality.

So, think easier thoughts about it.

Easier words.

Such as: "I am on a healing journey of my mind. It takes time, and
I am learning new things every day to grow into a better person."

Doesn't that sound so much better?

It's so much easier to do too, when you say it this way.

Try doing this in every hard situation; it will
give you a new perspective about it.

Day 72

How do you believe in yourself?

By loving and accepting yourself for who you are.

Accept that this is who you are, and that the universe put you on this path because it knew you could handle it.

You are on your own unique path.

Embrace it.

You have other qualities that other people don't have.

Stop trying so hard.

Stop trying to prove anything to anyone.

Be you.

Live and love your path and your life because there are things in it you need to see, hear, and enjoy.

You are a soul in a body.

Remember that.

Your true self is your soul, not your body.

Day 73

When you feel lost or depressed or unloved on your path, remember to feel the love and connection of God that is flowing to you, every minute of the day.

Embrace that.

Feel that.

Love that.

That unconditional love is what you're ignoring when you are depressed or lost.

That love is what you are not feeling when you are sad, down, and lonely.

That love is always there for you, always.

When you stop feeling the love of God, you feel negative emotions and can spiral deeper into depression.

You need to turn the other cheek, have a new perspective, and see the love and light of God.

This love takes you to happiness, bliss, joy, appreciation, and the list goes on and on.

Look at it, be it, and feel the love that is in you and around you.

Everywhere you go, happiness is there for you.

Connect to it again because that's where the true you is.

At one with God's unconditional love is where your real and true life is.

Day 74

The process of life is being satisfied in the moment.

It's the key to mastering anything and everything in your life.

Stop looking for it to be already here, and just enjoy
the journey getting to where you want to go.

That's the process of life.

If you keep thinking of your lack of something, then
that is what you will be manifesting into your life.

When you appreciate everything that you have and
love it, you will get more of that into your life.

That's how the process of life works.

So, look inside yourself and start asking what you feel like
you need right now and can't seem to stop wanting.

Probably money, a better job, a home, more love, more
clarity, a relationship, or anything you are desiring.

When you change your thoughts to appreciate and love the things
you have, then you will get more of those things on your path.

This is the process of life.

The best way to live life is on purpose.

To live deliberately and in the moment.

Set your intentions every day to appreciate and love life in all ways.

Including yourself.

Change your mindset, change your life.

Day 75

Your purpose in life is to create your life.

It is to create a life you love.

It is to live happily, and to live in joy and peace and bliss.

Your purpose in life is to find your passions.

Everyone has one that is unique to them.

Your purpose in life is to show others how to live this way.

Your purpose in life is to love others unconditionally.

Your purpose in life is to uplift others.

Your purpose in life is to be the best version
of yourself that you can be.

Your purpose in life is to awaken to the truth and
to live without resistance to the flow of life.

Your purpose in life is to have trust and faith
that God has your back every day.

It is your purpose in life to live in the moment.

This is every soul's purpose in the universe.

Day 76

Stop putting your happiness in other people's hands.

Stop letting the opinions of others affect who
you are and where you are going.

Stop blaming everyone else for how you are feeling.

When you blame others for their actions,
you are letting them control you.

You can only control you, and no one else.

You are not a victim here, but you are playing one.

Own up to your actions and learn from them.

Others are not responsible for your actions.

Start responding, not reacting, then you will start the healing process.

Nothing outside of you can hurt you; it is
your reaction to it that hurts you.

Day 77

We are born with pure, positive energy,

it is our birthright, and our soul right.

Fear is brought into us from the outside.

We are born with unconditional love.

We can't be both fear and love.

They are the exact opposites.

Everything we need is inside of us.

Love is in us.

Fear is outside of us.

And it is also an illusion.

Almost all of us live in fear.

So far away from our true self of love.

So, let go of fear today because fear is not who you are.

Love is.

Day 78

We all have the freedom to choose our life.

We all have the freedom to see new ways.

We all have the freedom to be better people.

We all have choices.

Freedom to choose is our right.

We can freely look at the bad, or we can freely
look at the good in any situation.

It's a free choice.

We are free to choose to see every situation in any way we like.

Good or bad.

Easy or hard.

Simple or difficult.

It's our choice how we see our life.

Our choices change our life and guide us to more
bad things or more goodness on our path.

If we choose to look at the bad in every situation, then
our life will get worse, and we will only see the bad.

The freedom of choice is ours.

Free will is a very powerful tool for us to use on our path.

Freedom to choose is ours.

Free will is in us.

So, use it to choose the good in your life, not the bad.

And use it to change your life and how you see it.

Day 79

It's easy to be happy.

Do things you love more often, like find your passions,
take a walk, change your words, and see the good
instead of the negative in people and situations.

Self-love and self-care are very important in changing your life.

Be aware of your thoughts, words, how you speak,
and what you focus your attention on.

It's not going to land in your lap.

You have to choose this every day to be happy.

If you don't choose it, you won't change.

Hard truth.

It's a choice to be happy and once you start to choose
to be happy, then it will become easier and easier.

It's up to you to choose to change.

No one else can do it for you.

Day 80

Affirm this:

Today in my life I am desiring a feeling of contentment.

I am happy with my life.

I am feeling full of love and light.

I am eager to see my life unfold.

I am positive, I am honest, and I am truthful.

I am good.

I am healthy.

I have faith in God, the universe, and source energy,
that life will keep getting better and better.

I love my life today and always.

I have all I need in my life to be happy and content.

My path in life is beautiful.

Day 81

Trust that your path will always take you where you
want to go, either the long way or the short way.

You will always get to where you are meant to be on either path.

Some take longer to learn, change, grow, and evolve.

Some learn the lesson quickly and move forward into the new.

It's your journey to take, so enjoy the ride.

It's never ending.

Trust your path, enjoy your path, and love your path.

It's all yours.

Day 82

The beginning is always today.

The new is here in every moment.

Every day is a new chance to step into our
truth and discover who you truly are.

You are here to create and enjoy every moment in your life.

You are here every day to create things you love.

You are here every day to help others on their
path and to co-create with them.

You are here every day to move forward into the new.

Every moment is new and in the now.

The only chance you have to live our fullest life is in
the now, today, and in the present moment.

Today is always a new beginning, so love it, live it, choose
it, be here in the now, and enjoy every moment.

$\mathcal{D}ay$ 83

Every time you praise yourself, you are uplifting
your soul and pushing back your ego.

Every time you compliment yourself, your ego is deflating.

Whenever you feel happy about yourself, you are ignoring your ego.

Self-love is the most important thing that you can do for yourself today.

Self-love helps heal your wounds and heal and soften your heart.

It helps you let go of your ego.

Being easy on yourself is important.

Being kind to yourself is important.

Your mindset will change to one of love and kindness and compassion.

Start doing this today and when you do, you will change your life.

Day 84

Negative emotions in your life come to show you change.

Negative emotions show you what you need to change in your life.

You feel negative emotions because you are turning your
love away from who you are and from the love of God.

God always loves you unconditionally.

When you are hurting, suffering, feeling guilt, shame, or
disappointment, you are not looking at yourself the way God sees you.

Negative emotions come to you to help you see what
you need to heal and change in your life.

They come to help you evolve, grow, and move forward.

Seeing the lesson in a situation changes how you see it and changes
you in the process. Negative emotions bring positive changes as you
move forward into the new awareness of the lessons on your path.

Day 85

Letting go of past hurts, forgiving yourself and others who have hurt you, allows you to move forward as a new you.

Letting go changes your life and will let in something new, amazing, and exciting.

It will be out of this world if you look forward with excitement at the new path opening for you.

It is so important to heal and let go.

Loving yourself on your path is the key to healing.

Without love inside you cannot love another.

Letting go helps you start to love yourself and accept yourself and your past.

Life starts when you love yourself now and let go of the past.

You can't change it.

Heal from it.

Don't look back because your new life is in front of you.

Day 86

You think you have control of this path that you are on, but you don't.

Your path is controlled by your soul, your higher self, and your life.

Your soul is the leader.

Your soul is in charge.

Your soul is leading you to your destiny.

Your soul is divinely guided always.

Your body and mind are following this destiny, but
you may not even be aware of this concept.

You may think you are in control.

And you are to an extent, but there is a bigger purpose, vision, and
intention for your life that your soul know and is guiding you to.

That is why there is the saying, "Follow your heart."

Because that is the guidance of the divine and your soul.

Following your heart brings you to everything you
are seeking and to the truth of who you are.

When you start to veer off the path of the bigger picture and
destiny for yourself, your soul or the universe pulls you back by
giving you resistance, negative emotions, and roadblocks.

Your soul is in charge of your journey.

You can choose to listen to your heart and
follow your soul's beautiful path.

Or you can choose to follow your ego, and you will have resistance,
roadblocks, detours, and negative emotions on your path.

And the hard road won't be as pretty.

You should always follow your heart, your passions, your talents, and your love because they are all connected to your divine path, life, and destiny.

Day 87

Everyone has a past; some we love, and some we don't.

If we can stop letting our past define us, we can change our life.

We can change who we perceive ourself to be in the present moment.

If we stop looking back at our past and only look
forward, we will change who we are.

The past only defines us if we let it.

We bring the past to the present moment every time we look at it.

We are now making the past the present and that is not who we are.

We are not the people we were the past but
the people we are in the now.

Don't let the past hurt you.

Don't let the past define you.

Let the present moment define your life
moving forward into the future.

That's where real life is.

Right now.

Day 88

Helping others helps us.

When we give our love to one another, we are spreading our vibration.

We help ourself feel our heart space and
mind by opening our love to them.

Every time we give love, we change their
vibration and ours a little more.

If we keep helping others, our vibration will rise, changing
us, and we will soon start to change our path.

Helping others helps change our world and their world for the better.

It's a win, win situation.

Day 89

Create peace inside of you.

Your energy is the only that you can control.

If you have peace inside of you, you will create peace around you.

If you are letting the world outside of you control you,
then your life will be affected inside of you.

The outside world is not who you are.

You can create a peaceful, loving path and life
if you focus on your own inner world.

Stop seeking outwardly and start seeking within you.

That's where you exist.

Nowhere else.

There is peace, love, and happiness within you.

Use them to create your life.

They are always there for you, and that is who
you truly are: peace, love, and happiness.

The Tranquil Ride

This is my favourite piece of artwork; it is so peaceful and relaxing.

I just want to spend the day in this canoe and explore
the lake and enjoy the peace and quiet ride.

I can be one with God and see the beauty that
has been created all around me.

It's Time to Believe in Yourself — 103

Day 90

We are always giving people labels, like artist,
mechanic, teacher, or doctor.

These are roles that we play, but they are just labels, not who we are.

Who we really are isn't a label.

We are spirits; we are souls; we are energy; we are the energy of God.

We are here to experience life on Earth.

We don't have roles; we just are.

Our bodies are a tool to help us experience, explore, and create our life.

We are the awareness that creates life.

We are the life force of the Creator.

We create for God to experience creation.

We are the creators for the energy of God, our Creator.

That's who we truly are.

Day 91

You are the light of the universe.

You came here to shine brightly.

You came here to light up the world with
the light of God inside of you.

You are pure energy, pure light, and the pure essence of God's energy.

You are here in this present moment to discover this light
inside of your heart and to shine it outward for all to see.

God is showing you this light everywhere you go, everywhere
you create, and everywhere you experience life.

Love is the light; it is in your soul, your body, your mind,
and it is in everyone to feel, to see, and to be.

The universe's energy is love and light.

Everyone is made of love and light so that each of us can create our life
in the eyes of that love and light and be aligned with God's energy.

Love yourself, others, life, animals, the planet, and the universe
because they are all made of this love and light too.

Everyone is created, and everything has God's energy in it.

Start to see the love and light within you, and you will change
your life, others' lives, the earth's life, and the universe's life.

You are love and light.

You are life, and you are creating it with God in
every moment for eternity together.

Day 92

Don't try to ignore the hurt inside of you.

Look, see, acknowledge, feel, and forgive it, then let it go.

You are not to blame others for it.

They are your wounds to heal.

They are showing you something that you
need to change inside of you.

If you don't acknowledge this pain and hurt, it will
continue to grow and affect your life even more.

It will control you.

It will move you backward.

It will show itself over and over again on your
path until you acknowledge it.

Not looking at your pain is unhealthy.

You will turn into a toxic person if you don't
see the wounds that need healing.

If you acknowledge your pain, by feeling, seeing, and forgiving
it, then letting it go right away, you will quickly be able to move
forward to a stronger, calmer, happier, easier, and more loving path.

Don't ignore what's hurting you.

Heal it, look after it, see it, and find the reason for the pain.

Let it go so that you can change that pain into happiness.

You will change your life by healing your
wounds instead of ignoring them.

Day 93

Having faith and trust in the unknown can be a challenge.

Having faith and trust sometimes can be scary.

If you live each day to the fullest and live each day happy,
you will keep the faith in what you don't know.

You don't have to know everything.

You can't.

Only God knows where you are going, what is coming to you, and
how you are going to receive whatever is for you on your path.

You need to be patient and let God guide you to it.

As you wait patiently for things to unfold, you can create
a beautiful life full of love, happiness, joy, and peace.

This is what you are truly here for.

Living this beautiful life that is guided by God is your true purpose.

God will surprise and delight you every day if you live on
this beautiful path of divine love, trust, and faith.

Have faith that there is always more to come.

Align your path with God's love.

Align your life with that unconditional love that God
streams to you every moment of your life.

Having faith is about trusting that God truly
knows you and is in your heart always.

You are in God's hands every day.

$\mathcal{D}ay$ 94

You have gone through so much in your life.

You have been down, and you have been up.

You have been down even deeper.

But you keep on going and seeing the light
that is on the other side of this.

You grow, learn, and evolve.

You take your power back.

You step into something so amazing and beautiful that you couldn't
even imagine when you were in that darkness on your path.

There is light guiding you to light.

And then there is even more light.

You find the light and the love of God.

You find your passions, purpose, and love for yourself in that light.

You find peace, happiness, and unconditional

love in that light.

You find others who help you on our way,
and you feel and absorb their love.

You change into the being you are supposed to be with all of
this love and light from God, the universe, and yourself.

The darkness can be deep, but the light will always
be the way to leave the darkness behind you.

The light makes you grow, love, evolve, and blossom into
beautiful soul that will light up your life and way.

Step into the light, God's light, that is here for you always.

Day 95

Affirm this:

I live in satisfaction of my life.

I appreciate all the goodness, kindness, knowing, love, compassion, beauty, ease, peace, and calmness that comes to me from that satisfaction.

It's a free feeling to know that I have all of that inside of me to access anytime I want it.

All I need and desire is here, and more is coming to me in divine timing.

I am ready in anticipation for what the universe has to surprise me with next.

I am eagerly following my path to everything I want.

It's all on its way to me.

Day 96

Change your words today.

Change your mindset today.

Change your thoughts today.

When speaking with criticism to others or yourself, you set a negative tone in your energy and vibration and get more of that back on your path.

Start speaking with love, compassion, and appreciation to yourself and others.

Say positive, encouraging, supportive, and loving words to everyone, including yourself.

When you change your words, you change your path, your energy, and vibration.

You change your life.

Day 97

You are very powerful when you are aware that you are
doing things out of old patterns and behaviours.

When you recognize this, that's real growth.

When you notice you are doing things that you
have the power to change, that's powerful.

Your life starts to change into a new version
of yourself, and that is amazing.

Your life and path will change dramatically.

Keep going, keep growing, and keep moving forward on your path.

$\mathcal{D}ay$ 98

When you are at peace with who you are and where you are going, you don't care what anyone thinks about you.

You now have a higher level of peace within yourself.

It's called self-worth, and when you have self-worth, you have everything you need.

Be confident, hold your head up high, and walk with a purpose.

Know who you are.

Know what you want on your path.

Don't seek validation from others; you have it inside of you.

You are made of that.

You are made of worthiness, confidence, and purpose.

Don't forget it.

Day 99

Life really is in this moment.

You have nothing going wrong, and everything is moving forward.

You're healing in this moment.

You're growing, changing, and evolving in this moment.

There is nothing going wrong.

It's all unfolding and happening as it should.

It's a process, and there is no end game.

Every day you are getting there little by little.

Day 100

That negative and fear-based voice in your head is your ego.

Stop listening to that voice.

Let it go.

Stop letting it control you.

Your true inner being is the voice in your head that is full of love, guidance, support, and wants to lead you somewhere amazing.

That is your soul talking to you.

Listen to that voice.

It is a quiet and gentle, not loud and annoying and in your face.

That's your ego.

Listen to your soul.

When you're in a happy place, feeling great, uplifted, and have little to no resistance to what is going on, you will hear that little voice.

Listen to it.

Follow it.

Your soul knows what you want, and it is guiding you to it.

Your ego thinks it knows what you want, but it makes you afraid of it and wants you to stay where you are.

When you drop that egoic voice, you will hear that inner being, your soul, speaking to you.

You are letting that voice in and hearing it when you are happy and raising your vibration.

So, the importance of happiness and a quiet
mind are essential in your daily life.

Meditation is the best way to quiet your mind so that you can
hear the messages that are intended for helping you in your life.

Day 101

If you are connected to source energy, the universe, God, or whatever you call your higher power, you are powerful.

We are all connected to this source.

You have the power to be, do, and have whatever you want.

You have the power to change your life.

It will also change others around you.

You are an uplifter to others.

You are pure, positive energy.

You are a creator.

You are amazing.

When you are connected to who you are, what you want, and where you are going, you are unstoppable.

Your power is all within yourself.

You create it, believe it, know it, and feel it.

You are one with your higher self, with God, and with the universe.

Connecting is the true power.

Knowing is the true power.

Being you is the true power.

Power comes from within.

Power isn't ever in the outside world.

Stop looking there.

Start looking inside.

If you believe it, know it, and feel it, you will have it.

Take your power back.

It's there for you every minute of your life.

Day 102

Nothing is impossible.

Nothing.

If you want it, you can achieve it.

The word impossible says, "I'm possible."

If you want to heal and move forward, you have to start
believing and knowing that everything is possible.

Each step you take gets you closer and closer
to what you are focussing on.

Stop focussing on what you can't do and focus on what you can do.

It will be impossible for anyone who thinks
negatively or thinks that something is hard.

Change takes time; it's a process.

Change doesn't happen overnight; it's gradual, so you might
not notice it right away, but one day you will see it.

You are doing this, and you are changing.

Change takes willpower, dedication, focus,
determination, and a positive mindset.

You are not perfect.

You will take steps backward and forward, but one day and one step
at a time, you will move forward into a new path and a new person.

Everything is possible.

Nothing is impossible.

Change is beautiful.

Change is messy at first, but once you can see
your wings coming out, you will fly high.

You will be beautiful and new.

You won't look back at who you once were because you will
want to see what's happening going forward onto a new path.

Day 103

Stop worrying about what could happen and start changing your perspective to look at it as what can happen.

Your life can be amazing, better, and beautiful.

It will be once you let go of that fear that is holding you back.

Fear doesn't let in the good.

Fear doesn't let your path flourish.

Fear doesn't let your mind grow.

Only when you start living out of love and happiness will your mind start to grow and change.

Let go of your fear and live your life today.

$\mathcal{D}ay$ 104

Affirm this:

Today and every day on my path, I ask for guidance,
help, support, and love from my angels, spirit guides,
ascended masters, ancestors, and God.

I know they are with me everywhere I go, but they will
not interfere on my path until I ask them to.

It's important that I ask for help every day.

My spirit guides will not infringe on my free will,
but they are always showing me the way.

When I ask for help, I give them permission to step in in a
beautiful way to help me in my day, in my life, and on my path.

They surround me everywhere I go.

I have an entourage of spirits and guides around me,
just waiting to help me as soon as I ask them.

They take great joy in helping me.

They are happy for me when I finally start to
acknowledge them and connect with them.

I am never ever alone on my path.

I know I have many angels and spirits surrounding me.

I feel this, and I see this.

They are here with me for eternity.

They love me unconditionally.

They know me, love me, and support me, and they
are there for me every step of the way.

Day 105

Your path is your path.

If you think you are struggling, you may be
moving forward and not even realizing it.

Stop looking at other people's path.

Their path is not your path.

Your path is your path.

Unique to you only.

Everyone moves and flows at different
awareness and conscious levels.

When you see what you need to do, you will move even faster.

The universe will provide you with circumstances that
will help you see what you need more clearly.

Then you can move forward.

Sometimes it takes more time for others to
see the clearer path ahead of them.

Everyone is going in the same direction, which is home
to God, but each person takes their own individual
path, journey, and adventures to get there.

No one else can live your life for you.

You need to experience these things in your own way, from
your own point of view, and from your own perspective,
in order to see the clearer path in front of you.

Day 106

You need to know that you are loved
by God every moment of the day.

Love is God.

You are love.

You are God.

If someone else is not seeing this, you can only be an
example and plant the seeds toward this love.

Others have to find their own way to love, and you can be
the way for them in the hopes that they will follow you.

They are in a process, just like you.

Be love and show them the way.

You can't change others, but you can be the example of it for them.

They will either have to join you or fall away.

You cannot join them at their level, as that is moving
backwards, and you can't look back on your path.

You have already been there.

You are not going that way.

You are living forwardly on your path.

Keep planting the seeds.

Keep showing love and being love.

It's the way to a better life, a better path, and a better you.

Day 107

Don't become attached to an outcome of something.

Learn to let go of things having to be a certain way.

That's conditional love.

Let things flow naturally and see where the universe takes you.

Let it unfold as it should.

If you resist and try to force outcomes to be the way
you want, you will get resistance on your path.

There will be forces trying to stop you.

Stop doing that.

That's what is stopping your life.

That's what is making you feel frustrated, angry, sad, hurt, etc.

That's what is giving you nothing but grief and heartache.

Stop being attached to an outcome in your life and path.

It is hindering your life.

You are in situations, circumstances, or meeting
people in your life for a reason.

If you are resisting, you are missing the beautiful path
ahead of you that you can't yet even imagine.

If you would only let go of your version of an outcome.

Attachment is what you need to let go of.

That will let your life flow easier and unfold as it should for you.

$\mathcal{D}ay$ 108

It's time to believe in yourself because that's
what you have to do in life.

You have to know that it is possible.

You have to believe you can do whatever you want to do.

You have to do the work.

No one else can do it for you.

Now is the time.

You need to stand up now and be a new person, with new
values, goals, passions, mindsets, and perspectives on life.

You are in your own way, with the limiting beliefs of failure,
fear, and your egoic mind making you feel powerless.

You are not powerless.

You are powerful.

Step into that power and let go of all the things
stopping you from believing in yourself.

Start today.

Believe in yourself.

You can do it.

Day 109

Life really is that simple.

It's love.

There is nothing else in the world that matters more than love.

Love your life.

Love your path.

Love everyone.

Love yourself.

Love changes everything.

Love changes you.

Love changes the world.

We are all made from this energy of love.

All of us.

God is the energy of love, and we are made of God's energy.

We are love.

When we live a life of love, we align with the energy of God.

Unconditional love.

If we would start to see that this is what we are made of and begin to love ourself the way God loves us, with that energy of love, we would change our life.

We would be in alignment with unconditional love.

Aligned with God.

We would change.

The world would change.

All we would feel, see, hear, taste, smell, and
know would be love all around us.

Love truly changes everything.

Love changes us into something beautiful.

Love would change the world into something beautiful and amazing.

It would be a beautiful world to live in.

Love makes the world go around.

Love is truly who we all are.

Day 110

Affirm this:

Happiness is what I live for every day.

It is in me to be happy.

Happiness is what I spread every day.

It is in me to give to others as well.

Happiness is what I feel every day.

Happiness is in me to feel every day.

Happiness is everywhere I go.

It is all I see.

Happiness is in each and every one of us.

Even me.

Happiness is a choice, and I choose to be happy every day.

Day 111

Give forgiveness to yourself, others, and the situation
that you are having a hard time letting go of.

You need to take the lessons that you learn from
these experiences and let the rest go.

This is why things happen to you.

You need to learn lessons in life and move forward,
or you will be stuck, and you won't grow.

And that will hurt you.

To just be stagnant in life, to be living in fear, hate,
anger, and frustration is hurting you so much.

You are meant to grow.

People, relationships, jobs, and experiences are here for a purpose.

They are here to help you learn from your
mistakes and keep you going forward.

You are not meant to dwell on them and feel bad about yourself.

You need to forgive yourself, then let it go.

Forgive others and thank them for showing you a
new path, a new view, and a new way to be.

Forgiveness allows you to feel peace, love, and happiness again.

It's the biggest step in healing your heart, mind, and soul.

Day 112

Your past isn't who you are.

Don't let your past define you.

It's gone.

And it's not who you truly are.

You are who you are in this present moment.

The past shapes you and you learn and grow
from it, but you are not your past.

You are who you are now.

In this moment.

Let go of the past that you think is you.

Forgive the past, let it go, and be free of it forever.

This allows you to breath in the new and all that comes with it.

New experiences come in when you don't look
back at who you think you were.

Be free and excited to flow forward into what today is bringing you.

Day 113

Give yourself some time to rest in your day.

You need a time for silence.

Just sitting and being.

When you sit and just be, without thoughts about who
you are or what you have to do, you will find peace.

This is meditation.

This is where your true self is.

In this silence is where you will find the true you.

Allow your true self to speak to you.

Hear the guidance from your higher self and your higher power.

It's a quiet, loving voice of guidance on your path.

You can listen to the guidance; it comes from
within you, when you are still and silent.

Sometimes you can't hear that inner voice because
of all the noise going on around you.

You can't focus on yourself because you are always listening outwardly.

Peace, joy, happiness, and love all come from within.

When you allow yourself time to sit in meditation, you will
find that inner peace, happiness, joy, and love for yourself.

This can truly help you to move through your
day more calmly and peacefully.

When you allow time for rest, silence, going within, and to know
your true higher self, you will change your path and you.

Sit, rest, and unplug every day.

Make time for you, to do this in your day, every day.

You will see your mental and physical health improve as well as your life and path moving forward, if you start practicing meditation every day.

Meditation, with no thoughts or actions, just sitting in the stillness and the silence, finding who you truly are and connecting with your higher self, is a very powerful, life-changing tool that should be done by everyone, every day.

Meditation changes your life.

Day 114

Strong or weak?

Which one are you?

You can't be both because they are two opposing emotions.

A person is strong because they are focussing on their strengths, their passions, their purpose, and their love for life.

A person is weak because they are focussing on their weaknesses and fears.

You can't be both.

Pick one.

Are you strong or weak today?

Where's your focus?

Hopefully strength.

Day 115

Today look forward to what is coming next.

Life gets better and better every day.

The more life we live, the more we learn and grow
from past experiences, and the more we let go of toxic
behaviours that we picked up along the way.

Today let go of toxic situations, people, and environments.

This is resistance on our path.

Let go and see what beautiful things come when we do.

Let go and be free of it.

Because letting go makes room for the desires, dreams,
abundance, and happiness that we want in our life.

We need to stop holding on to the toxicity and the hurt and the pain.

Just let it all go, and let it crash and burn.

We need to walk with our head up high, with a smile, and
keep moving forward toward new and exciting paths.

Day 116

Happiness is a decision, not an experience.

If you decide to be happy without what you thought
you needed to be happy, you will be.

Your experience is the result of the decision
to be happy, not the cause of it.

Choose happiness.

It is the better path and life.

Day 117

Every day is about trust and faith and letting your guidance system lead you on your path.

Be happy and love your life.

The universe will guide you to wherever you want to go and to whatever you want to do and be.

Let go of control, and let your desires lead your way.

Let your heart lead your path.

That's the key to a happy life.

That's the key to life.

Trust.

Love.

Joy.

Happiness.

Day 118

Living in the now is the solution to letting go of your problems.

Awareness.

Letting go.

When something arises in the moment, you can be aware of a problem and find a solution in the now moment.

Is it the truth?

Is it real?

You can make different choices.

When you live in the now, you can see a different perspective.

Meditation can help.

A quiet mind helps you to hear solutions.

When you see them show up you can be aware and make better decisions in the moment when they arise.

Living in the now helps us to see solutions to the problems on our path, and they become clearer as we quiet our mind and go within to seek the solutions that we need.

Day 119

What do you love about yourself today?

Self-love is the most important step to start
healing, growing, and changing.

How you treat yourself shapes your life.

When you put yourself down, you see a negative
life and path that steers into that reality.

When you praise yourself and love yourself unconditionally
for who you are, your path steers in a positive direction.

Would you talk down to your friends and family?

No, you try to uplift them.

Do that for yourself.

The first step in change is the biggest step to
having a better life and a better you.

Start speaking to yourself with kindness, love, and compassion.

Be your own best friend.

Day 120

Are you reacting or responding to others?

Reacting is a knee jerk action to something
you get offended about easily.

It's a trigger.

A trigger means this is where you need to heal
and work on your inner self more.

A response is a pause, a thought before you speak.

Taking a moment to question if something is true, and
if it is it helpful or hurtful before we respond.

Are you easily triggered?

Or do you pause and then respond out of love and kindness.

Be honest with yourself because it's where you need to
change and heal if you react to situations or people.

Solitude

I made this piece when I was alone on my path.

I was healing from my past and letting go of the old me and my old life.

This painting was painted while I was in solitude during COVID.

It was the first lockdown we experienced, and I was on my own
to find my way in the darkness and back into the light.

I was in the unknown, and I was finding
the new me inside this solitude.

It was transforming me and showing me a new
person, one I had never met before.

I was turning into a new person in this solitude.

I am forever changed because of COVID, and
my life will never be the same.

It's Time to Believe in Yourself — 141

Day 121

I have faith that whatever happens to me in my day, I will know what to do, and I will be able to make aware, conscious choices.

The universe will help me in guiding me in my decisions.

I will feel the positive and the negative
emotions attached to each experience.

I know whatever I choose, the universe will guide me through the obstacles and rejoice with me in the bliss moments.

My faith stands strong with the universe.

The universe has my back all the way to eternity.

Day 122

Shine your light bright today.

You are unique, and you are beautiful.

Don't let someone dim your light.

Shine it on others.

Let them see you glow.

Light up your own path.

Light up your own mind.

Light up your own life.

When others see you shining bright, you will
inspire their light to shine brighter too.

Have a bright day.

Day 123

Maybe you are wondering what your
purpose is here in this universe.

What is it?

How do you find it?

Follow your heart.

Your purpose in life is to create a life you love.

To be happy, and to live in peace and joy.

To live in unconditional love as the universe sees
you, as God sees you and loves you.

Your purpose in life is to be happy from within yourself.

When you do this, you send out unconditional love
to others, help others, and serve others.

You are here to help others and guide them as well on your path.

Everyone is in this universe together, as one, as equals.

When you help and love others without expectations, you
get back so much abundance from the universe.

You also have passions, sometimes many, which can help you to
make the universe a better place to be in, in some way or form.

To add to the love that is already flowing in the universe.

Your passions make your heart sing and when your heart
sings, you are emitting out more love to the world, adding
to the love that is already flowing in the universe.

Your purpose is to be happy, to create in alignment with the universe
and God's love, to live in love with one another, and to help others.

Everyone is equal in the universe.

All made of love.

Follow your heart.

It's the way to your purpose.

Day 124

Every minute that goes by is gone.

You cannot change it.

You keep dwelling on mistakes you have made and regretting your past.

You forget that life is in the now.

Learn from the past so that you can create an
even more beautiful life moving forward.

If you are appreciating the now and learning from the
past, you will have a better life moving forward.

Life is now, so start seeing and living in the now.

The past is gone, and we cannot undo or change it.

Accept and learn from it, and let it go.

Stop looking back and dwelling on your past.

Start loving what you have now and what else is coming to you.

Life is now.

Every minute you waste looking at the past, you miss
out on the now and beauty that is in front of you.

Don't waste the beauty of the now moment.

Love it and live it.

Day 125

If you look at your path and see patterns to the timelines
and connections you have made, they all came to you
just when you needed someone or something.

Everything happens at the perfect time for you to
learn, experience, grow, and move forward.

If you don't go through these things, you will
experience them again at a different time.

The universe wants you to awaken to unconditional love, to
open your mind, and to let go of fear, worry, and negativity.

Knowing that you are here to create your life in the eyes of
God, to stop suffering, to let go of your past, and to not worry
about what is coming next, you can surrender to the now.

The universe is showing you these signs every day to enlighten
you to wake up to the truth and to knowing the process of life.

You are here in body to create a life of love.

You are here to live unconditionally in love with
life, with yourself, and with others.

You are here to be positive and to know that
everything you want, and desire is given to you by the
universe and God, when you are ready for it.

Be ready.

It is coming, and when you start to wake up to unconditional
love, all that you want will flow into you.

Day 126

You attract what you are.

You attract who you are.

You are powerful.

You are energy.

You are vibration.

You are a creator.

What you are focussing on, you attract.

When you let go of what you are focussing on, it moves
away from the reality that you are creating.

What's in your life at this moment is what
you have attracted into your reality.

Your mind is the most powerful thing in our life.

Be aware of your mindset.

Be aware of your thoughts.

Be aware of your focus.

Be aware of your feeling and emotions.

Be aware of everything because you are in
the driver's seat of your own life.

Day 127

Appreciation is the highest form of love.

It tops gratitude.

Appreciation comes from a place of satisfaction.

You are satisfied with your life, your path, who you are, your job, your family, etc.

You don't need anything else in your life.

You are appreciating everything you have.

When you appreciate what you have and where you are going, then you're ready for more to come into your life.

You will receive more in your life because you appreciate everything in your life.

If you want more money, appreciate what you have in this moment and watch the universe bring you more abundance into your life.

What are you appreciating in your life today?

Day 128

When you are trying to change or break old habits and patterns, you really need to change your words to better, positive, uplifting ones.

Start saying things with softer and lighter words.

Look for a positive perspective for something that isn't working.

If you are someone who is worrying and living in fear, instead of saying, "I can't do this. I have tried everything, but nothing works," say this:

"I am finding new ways of looking at my life and new awareness in my mind. I am seeing the good in every situation and letting go of the worry and the fear. I am moving forward into a new peace and ease in my mind, and I feel calmness instead of fear. I can change my mind, and I can change my life."

Doesn't that sound better?

Change your words, vibration, and energy to be softer, easier, and calmer so that you will attract the same back.

What you say and feel affects your reality.

Be aware of your vibration and your words because the universe is hearing them and sending you back everything you are vibrating at it.

Day 129

Taking action isn't always the best thing.

Sometimes you need to relax and let things unfold
the way they should, so you can see and feel what
to do next in the moment when things arise.

Trust and faith.

Not action and force.

Let things flow to you naturally and let the
resistance of forcing things go.

Inspired action is the best action.

When you genuinely feel the urge to move, then move and go.

Otherwise, relax, chill, be happy, and have fun.

Day 130

If you feel stuck in a situation or are living
in fear, these are signs for change.

The universe will make your life so uncomfortable and
hard that you will be forced to move forward.

It will force you out of your comfort zone and into the
new because you have been resisting the signs for so
long that you need to move into a new path.

Change and growth are necessary in life to evolve and
to experience new things that are waiting for you.

So, if you are in a spot right now where you are fighting
change, you won't be able to resist it forever.

The universe will show you that new path and move you
toward it, and you will have to face the change.

Change is a good thing; it is not something
to fear but something to embrace.

It makes your life better again.

It helps you out of the old behaviours and patterns.

It helps you see clearly again.

It helps you find yourself again.

The universe is always guiding you and
bringing you where you need to be.

The timing that things happen will always be perfect
for you to learn and grow and move forward.

Everything happens for a reason.

There are no coincidences.

Have faith and trust that the universe always has your back.

Day 131

The universe is always guiding us and
bringing us where we need to be.

The timing that things happen to us is always perfect
for us to learn and grow and move forward from.

Everything happens for a reason.

There are no coincidences in life.

We need to have faith and trust that the
universe always has our back.

It is taking us where we need to be all the time.

Follow the signs.

We lead with our heart to the path
that the universe is taking us on.

Day 132

Your well-being is something you should never ignore.

You make time to be unhappy, sad, depressed, to feel unworthy, to dwell on the past, and to live in anger and frustration.

These feelings are choices.

You are making a choice to be this way.

Start focussing on your mental well-being by choosing love, happiness, joy, positivity, bliss, contentment, excitement, etc.

These are your natural states of pure, positive energy.

It is who you are.

You keep choosing who you are not.

Start choosing your well-being because it's flowing to you naturally and easily.

Start being your true you.

Choose it, and you will change your life.

Day 133

Always put yourself first.

Don't lose yourself for someone else.

It's not worth it.

You can only fix yourself.

You are the most important person in your life.

Don't forget that.

You have to live with you forever, so live for you.

Love your life, your path, and who you are.

Don't let anyone tell you anything different.

It's not their life.

It's yours.

Live for you.

Day 134

You have to be alone to heal fully.

You cannot focus on you and someone else at the same time.

You can't heal in the same place or with
the same person that broke you.

It takes time and dedication to see where you are
hurting and what needs to be healed.

Being alone is a superpower.

Once you realize this is what you have to do, you will
start to heal and grow as you make time to be alone
with yourself and begin processing your emotions.

Healing is work and time and dedication on your path.

When you do it, you will transform into a beautiful new
person, someone you will love unconditionally.

Day 135

What is life about?

Being positive and letting more of that in.

It's about learning from mistakes and taking
the lessons with us into the new.

It's about being better every day.

It's about creating a life that you love with people you love in it.

Life is about your passions and your purpose
and moving your life toward that.

It's about following your heart, not living in fear.

Life is about growing, changing, being new, and
learning about who your true self is again.

It's about enjoying the little things that make you happy.

Life is for happiness, joy, love, and compassion.

If you have those qualities in your heart, your life
will show it and bring you more of them.

Joy, peace, happiness, and unconditional love
are truly in you and in your life.

Day 136

You need to start accepting how things are.

Stop trying to force things to be a certain way.

People, life, and relationships change.

Accept it.

Grow from it.

Learn from it.

Move forward because of it.

Acceptance of what is takes away the resistance
and lets things flow as they should.

You cannot control how things go things.

You cannot make things be how you want them to be.

Accepting means letting go of what was and what will be
and seeing people, situations, and relationships for what they
are, letting them flow the way they are supposed to.

Everything in your life happens for a reason.

You need to see that, accept that, and know that.

Accept what is in front of you and stop trying to
make it different than what it truly is.

$\mathcal{D}ay$ 137

It's not your problem or place to judge people.

It's not your place to shame people and to put them down.

Don't judge people on their looks, race, colour,
sex, religion, occupation, health, etc.

Because you don't know them, their path, or their life.

You are labelling and shaming them for their life and path.

No one is better than you or anyone else in this universe.

No one.

Stop putting people down, insulting them,
having cruel thoughts, and judging.

It's enough.

The world has had enough.

The world needs better.

The world needs kindness, love, and compassion.

Everything else is a lie.

Treat everyone equally because everyone is equal.

You are one with each person in the universe.

In this world together.

Start showing it and acting like it.

Day 138

Faith is believing in yourself.

You are one with God, the energy of the universe.

When you believe in yourself, you are showing
that you have faith in yourself.

The universe shifts for you when you have the intention to
change and believe and know that you can be better.

And have faith in God's energy because you
are connected to that inside of you.

You are always connected.

What you believe is what you will see on your path.

Make sure you have faith that you can do anything,
and the universe will show you that you can.

You are connected always.

You are one.

You are one with God.

Day 139

Keep working on yourself today.

Let go of your past, your future, and live in the moment, loving yourself, your life, and your path.

Embrace love, not fear.

Fear is an illusion.

Self-care, meditation, being in nature, choosing yourself over things you do not want to do.

Live for your passions and do them with love.

Believe in yourself today.

Love yourself today.

Be your best self today.

Day 140

We are created to create.

We are created to love.

We are created to show others love.

We are created to be abundant.

We are created to live in peace.

We are created to live as one.

We are created equally.

We are created to be.

There is no suffering, shaming, guilt, or unworthiness in us.

Let it all go and be who you are meant to be.

We are made in the eyes of God.

We are God.

Let's start living like that today.

Day 141

You cannot separate from God.

When you feel separate from him, you are
not looking at God's love for you.

It's always there, forever and for eternity.

God walks with you everywhere, every day.

God is your partner in life.

God is inside of you.

God is in every person, creature, plant, insect, etc.

God is in everything made by you.

God created you so that he could experience
whatever you do here on your path.

When you turn away from God's love, you are out of alignment.

When you love yourself, you are loving
God as well.

You are in alignment with his love.

This is why you feel separate from

God.

You are out of alignment with him when you feel
negative emotions, pain, and suffering.

God is always in a state of unconditional
love, and he never wavers from it.

But you are always moving from states of love,
anger, anxiety, fear, happiness joy, hate, etc.

These things cause you to be out of alignment
with God's state of unconditional love.

And this is why you feel alone, depressed, or sad.

Remember this the next time you feel disconnected from God.

God's love doesn't stop being unconditional, but
you have to move to meet him at that level.

God will never move from that state for you.

Universal love is the truest state of all.

It's pure alignment and oneness with everything.

Being in alignment changes your life.

Day 142

Your body listens to every word you say to it.

Your body then reacts to everything you say to it.

It starts to shift to whatever you are telling it.

So, if you say you're stupid, your body shows that to you.

If you say you are smart, your body shows that to you.

If you say you are ugly, your body will reflect that to you.

If you say you are beautiful, your body will reflect that to you.

The cells in your body are listening to everything you tell it.

Your appearance is a part of your mindset.

If you have a low vibration, living in your egoic mind and negativity, then you will be fatigued, age quicker, have aches and pains, and disease and mental disorders will be present.

If you have a higher vibration, full of unconditional love, self-worth, self-love, beauty, and internal happiness, you will radiate beauty from within.

You will start to look younger, feel younger, and your aches and pains will disappear.

Your mental health will improve dramatically.

Your anxiety and depression will fall away.

You will have inner peace, joy, and happiness.

What you tell your body affects your life.

It's listening and responding.

It's changing its cells for you.

It's conscious and aware.

So, think before you speak negatively about yourself.

It changes your life.

Day 143

We all have gifts.

These gifts are ours, and they are a part of us.

Our gifts are given to us after lifetimes of shedding our ego
and learning lessons that we need to live on this planet.

When we arrive at this point, we have no karmic lessons to
learn, and we are living our life out of love, not ego.

Our gifts start to awaken in us.

We all have them inside of us.

Every one of us.

We need to learn, grow, and to receive them.

We are on a path that we have to evolve from
in every lifetime we have lived.

To shed our ego is the way to opening them.

This is the path of awakening and enlightenment.

This is where everyone is headed.

Home to our highest, truest self.

It's a journey.

This is not inherited; it is truly who we are.

This lifetime is for us to be enlightened, and so many are
awakening to these spiritual gifts that they have inside of them.

Gifts of seeing, knowing, hearing, healing, intuition,
visions of the future, just to name a few.

These gifts can become stronger and stronger.

These gifts are ours to use for good, to give back to others.

We all have them in some way.

They open when we are ready.

We have worked many lifetimes to open up these gifts.

We are moving to enlightenment on this earth.

It's going to be a truly amazing path for all of us.

Day 144

We are one with everything.

The universe, source energy, life force, God, is in everything that
we are, in everything we make, build, grow, see, feel, touch, etc.

There isn't one thing that this energy is not in.

We are made with love, the universal love of God.

That's what we are.

Love.

Let's start showing the earth, animals, and others
that we are here together in unity to help everything
in the universe flourish, grow, and be more.

We can all have what we need on this planet if we each see that we
are connected as one system of consciousness, energy, and vibration.

We are all connected forever in this realm and in
the spiritual realms on other planets as well.

Start to see this and feel this and know this.

We will change who we are, and we will
change the earth and the universe.

This is the way of life.

Day 145

Self-love is the start of the healing process.

To choose something negative, while putting your mindset, self-worth, self-love, and self-respect last, is a toxic pattern.

It's a behaviour that is running your life.

If you don't love yourself fully and choose yourself over the toxic relationships, the alcohol, the drugs, and the negative choices, you will never stop these toxic patterns.

You have to choose yourself first over all of that.

You have to realize that the love for your body, your mindset, your path, your higher self, and for God are the most important things you can choose to do for yourself on your journey.

You have to choose it.

Every day.

It's a choice.

And no one can help you in making that choice but you.

By doing the things you love.

Eating healthy.

Getting exercise.

Journalling your thoughts.

Meditation.

Speaking kindly about yourself, uplifting yourself, and forgiving yourself and others.

Gratitude and appreciation for your life, for what you have, and for the people in your life.

Choosing these things instead of toxic ones will change your life.

This has to be an everyday thing.

Not just when you hit rock bottom.

Every day.

It has to be a way of living and being.

When you are in a great mindset and space, you still have to continue to do this work every day.

Self-love needs to be a choice every day.

Day 146

You want the good life, but you are always looking at the bad.

You want more in your life, but you are always seeing what is missing.

You love others in your life, but you don't always love yourself.

Love is where it all starts.

Love what you have.

Love the good things in your life.

You included.

Love you, your life, and your path.

Love is everywhere and in everyone.

Love is life.

Day 147

Affirm this:

I am stepping into the new me.

I am stepping into a new awareness.

I am stepping into the next level on my path.

I am stepping into my power and my gifts and
into alignment with my true self.

My path is shifting, growing, expanding, and evolving.

I am aligning with God's unconditional love.

I am always walking my path with God, who is showing me the way.

This path is now lighting up for me with God's light and my light.

It's so bright and beautiful.

God's energy is everywhere.

God's energy is in me.

God's energy is in you.

Brighten your path by aligning with that love of God.

God's energy is everywhere for you to see and feel.

Step into that light of God.

It's in you and me and everyone around us.

Everyone is lit up with light and the love of God every day.

$\mathcal{Day}$ 148

Affirm this:

I am leading my life by my guidance system.

I am letting life come to me.

I am surrendering to the universe.

The universe knows what I want and desire.

It's guiding me there.

I won't let my ego guide me.

It goes nowhere but to disappointment.

I often think I know what I want because my ego has told me.

But I know that my ego is wrong almost every time.

My higher, inner voice is always right.

It will lead me to love, peace, happiness, truth, and to delightful surprises that I can't even imagine.

Sometimes I think I know what I want.

I have attachments to things, people, and situations in my life, which I know is my ego.

If I drop these attachments, I can let my guidance flow through me and lead me to so many beautiful things, ideas, and people that I didn't even know existed.

Flowing and surrendering is the true way of living.

Not knowing what's next is truly beautiful.

The universe wants me to have everything I desire.

It truly does.

I know that trust, faith, surrender, ease and flow, and living in the moment are truly the best life.

I need to let it go.

Surrender.

And see what surprises are waiting for me on my path.

Day 149

We all have toxic traits.

But this isn't who we are.

We all have an ego that we listen too, and it makes us believe that is who we are.

If we believe our ego is who we are, then we definitely have work to do to change.

We are not our ego.

We are love.

The ego has no love in it, only fear.

So, look at yourself deeply, at who you truly are inside.

Love, peace, happiness, joy, and bliss are who you truly are.

The ego tells you something different.

Look for those qualities and change.

That's your true self, not something negative.

Anything positive is the true self given to you when you were born.

This is who you are.

You need to find it inside of you and discover your truest self again.

Day 150

The path to awakening is a process that
takes time and is never ending.

Spiritual awakening is coming home to God, to the
truth of who you are and why you are here.

It's the path of truth.

It's the path to enlightenment.

It's the path after you have learned all your life and karmic lessons.

Earth is a school for you to learn, grow, and evolve,
and it takes many, many, many lifetimes to get to
this path of awakening and enlightenment.

You are here, and you are on that path.

It takes time, work, letting go of your ego, and
surrendering to the now and to the universe.

Meditation, healing, letting go, forgiveness, love, self-
love, and more are involved in awakening.

It takes trust and faith that what is yours will come to you.

It's unfolding in divine timing.

It takes surrendering, not suffering.

Your gifts are here for you now, so listen to your inner voice
and guidance system, your heart, and your intuition, and
they will lead you to the path that you need to be on.

This is the awakening process.

It's an everyday practice and over time, you
will change and be different.

Over time, you will look back and see that you were
evolving, changing, and moving forward.

Stop looking for it outside of yourself.

It's not there.

It's inside of you and you only.

Stop comparing your path and journey to others.

Everyone is different and unique.

Awakening is a path, and it is unfolding as you go.

Keep living every day, surrendering to the moment.

Trust, have faith, surrender, and let go of the old.

It's happening to you, within you.

Let it unfold.

Day 151

Start doing something for yourself today.

Take time out for you.

You're always giving, but this is now time for you to receive.

To recharge.

To rest.

To relax.

It's your turn to enjoy something you love.

Make yourself a priority.

Self-love changes your life.

What are you doing in your day that you love?

When you start to do things you love, you begin to look after yourself.

You start to love life again, and you want to enjoy it
because you now love your path and yourself.

You want better for yourself.

You can see your addictions and change them.

You start to change because you love yourself so much that you
don't want to keep hurting yourself over and over again.

Self-love changes your life.

Over time you change your life to live out of love instead of hate.

Self-love not only changes your life, it saves it.

Cardinals in Love

I truly love cardinals.

They are messengers from the spiritual realm.

They are loved ones that have passed, showing
us a sign that they are with us.

They are beautiful birds with a beautiful song.

When I see a cardinal, I think of my grandmother.

Who do you think of when you see a cardinal?

Day 152

The universe doesn't make mistakes.

God knows what he is doing.

We are all here for a reason and a purpose.

We are all here to shine.

We are all here to show our talents and to
share our gifts with everyone.

We are all intertwined.

We are all connected.

We all fit together like a puzzle.

We have a bigger picture to serve in the universe.

We all play a part.

Don't ever think you don't fit.

You do.

There are no missing or extra pieces in this grand universe.

We all fit.

We are all one.

We are all loved equally, and we are all receiving love from
the universe every second of every day for all of eternity.

The universe is perfect.

God has made us the way we are so that we can share
our unique gifts and talents with each other.

We can help each other with our gifts, and we can help God with them, by creating even more love in the universe.

We are here for this.

We are here to shine.

Let's shine our light for the universe to see.

Day 153

Today when you think something feels scary,
remember God is with you.

God is guiding you and wants the best for you.

God leads you to the best things in life.

Going out of your comfort zone can be scary, but you need
to step into the unknown in order to change and grow.

You have to step into our courage and be brave today.

You need to know that you have something
bigger than us guiding you on your path.

You need to feel that and have faith and trust that
everything is going to work out and be ok.

God gives you everything you need on your
path to experience in your life.

It will come to you if you let go of your fear, which is your
ego, and step into the path of trust and faith in God.

Courage is moving forward, trusting, evolving,
and loving where you are going.

Fear can stop you.

Faith can move you.

Have faith, not fear.

Have love, not doubt.

God is here for you.

Surrender your fear to God and start living
the life he has planned for you.

Day 154

Keep moving forward.

Don't look back.

You made a good choice for yourself.

Stick to it.

Change will come as you move forward on a new path.

It may hurt for a minute, but you will have a lifetime
of good for choosing a new and better path.

You may not see it now because of fear, but don't let that stop you.

Your ego is telling you to be afraid of new things.

Let your ego go.

Let your intuition and love help you to keep looking forward.

Change is good.

Change is necessary in life.

Get going, and it will get better and better for you on your path.

Day 155

Start raising your vibration.

Start letting go of the old energy so that you can
live in the new energy of this earth.

Everyone can make a difference in this world right now.

It's up to everyone to change, to heal, to be new, and to find
their true self so they can be authentic and live a better life.

Live in the present moment.

Not the past.

Not the future.

Being in the now is important.

It's here for you now.

Life is in this moment.

So, raise your consciousness.

Change your energy, your life, and the world.

Day 156

You can only change yourself.

Not others.

Stop believing this.

Stop staying with people who are not going to change.

Start living for you.

Start healing for you.

Start being new for you.

You are all that you have.

Your life is for you.

You are worth it.

Keep moving forward.

You may lose relationships and friendships when you change, but you will find new friends and relationships that are healthy and loving.

When you discover who you really are, your life will shift.

You are here to create your own life, not someone else's.

You are here to be happy, positive, and full of love.

Start changing today.

Start seeing the truth and a new life to create for you.

$\mathcal{D}ay$ 157

Change affects everyone around you.

Growth affects everyone around you.

When you change in either direction, the universe shifts to your vibration, your intention, and to the energy you are sending it.

People that come into your life are directly because you are shifting and changing.

Be aware of who you are affecting in your life when you change.

They are too.

Change positively so that you can also have a ripple effect on the surroundings in your life.

Day 158

Everyone has their own perspectives in life.

You need to be open to new perspectives.

Your perspectives are unique to you.

Your perspectives resonate with your own path.

Your perspectives are not the same as anyone else's because everyone has had their own experiences.

You need to awaken to new perspectives and experiences that can change what you perceive to be the truth.

If you are close-minded to new perspectives, then you cannot have new ways of seeing things.

Being open-minded to new experiences will help you to grow consciously, to change, and to evolve to a higher awareness on your path.

If you are close-minded and can't see beyond your own views, you become stuck in your old patterns, old routines, and you don't move forward.

Perspectives challenge your limiting beliefs so that you can discover and know the truth.

The truth of the universe, your purpose, your path, and who you truly are.

Be open to seeing something new that may help change your life for the better.

Day 159

When we have negative emotions, it's because we are
not seeing or feeling the love that we are made of.

We are love, and anything other than that is showing us that we
are not in alignment with the feeling of that love in the moment.

Question the feeling and ask why, how, and what about it.

Stop.

Ask.

Pause.

Discover the truth in the feeling that need to
be seen in order to move through us.

Being aware of our emotions will help us move forward on our path.

We can't ignore these feelings, or they will just come back over and
over until they are looked at, felt, acknowledged, and then let go of.

It's ok to feel.

We must feel.

It's how we learn and change and grow into someone new.

We need to feel our emotions in the moment and be
aware of them so that they don't come back even bigger,
needing to be released the next time around.

This is how we heal.

This is how we move forward.

This is how we break patterns.

And this is how we love ourself even more.

Healing allows more love to flow to you, and
that love changes you and heals you.

Day 160

Appreciation is the highest form of love.

What do you appreciate in your life?

You may appreciate your health, well-being, family, friends, grandchildren, job, passions, creations, and life.

It is amazing that with everything we have, we don't really think about it.

We have so much abundance.

We don't have to be wealthy to be rich.

When we see the blessings in our life, our heart fills up with love and appreciation, and we don't feel like we need anything.

This is where happiness resides.

This is where life resides.

In our heart, full of appreciation and gratitude for all that we have within us.

Life is inside our heart.

It is there for everyone.

Find it.

Feel it.

Embrace it.

Love it.

Day 161

The mindset of knowing that you can do
and be anything is powerful.

No doubts, just knowing.

The universe changes for you with that mindset.

There is no fear only love with this mindset.

Our mindset makes us who we are.

If we have no fear, we are on a powerful
path of creating the life we want.

Day 162

Helping others helps you.

It changes you.

It helps you to feel love and helps others to feel love as well.

When you give with no expectation that is unconditional love.

When you give with expectation that is conditional love.

Unconditional love helps you to heal and to grow your
heart space, making room for more love to come in.

The more you give, the more you receive.

The less you expect in return from giving, the more you grow
into a loving person that lives from your heart space.

You are here to help, give, and receive from the universe.

You are here to show others that you love unconditionally
so that they can feel your love toward them.

Don't ask what's in it for you.

There is always something in it for you, and that is love from God
for helping spread universal love, kindness, and compassion.

That's how you change the world, by helping others on their path and
spreading love, joy, and peace to everyone you meet on your path.

Day 163

We are all connected.

To each other and to nature.

The earth is our home, and we are a part of this earth.

We are one with earth.

When we start to see that we are one with the earth, each other, and with the animals, maybe we will start treating everything and everyone better.

We are the earth.

We are connected with everything and everyone.

We are all one.

We are all connected.

Day 164

We can't change other people, only ourself.

We can influence the people around us with our actions and our words.

That's all we can do.

We can do our part by showing others the way to live.

That's our purpose.

Everything is as it is for a reason.

That has a purpose as well.

We are not here to change the world.

We are here to change ourself.

That changes the world we live in.

That's a ripple effect to create change.

We start to change ourself, our surroundings, and the people around us.

That's what we can do to help change the world.

Change us.

Day 165

You have to look at what you truly believe in.

You could be wrong.

If you are that's a limiting belief.

It's limiting your life and what comes into it.

What you believe is how you live and how you see the world.

If your mind is closed to new ways and perspectives, it will hinder you from changing, growing, and evolving.

Like if you believe in God or not.

Life if you believe money is hard to come by.

Like if you believe you are not worthy of happiness.

All of this change is how you view the world.

Your world.

If you can't see things differently, then you will never change.

Open your mind to new perspectives, new ways, new thoughts, and they may change your life for the better.

A closed-mind stops you, while an open-mind takes you to new and amazing places.

Ask yourself what you believe that might be hindering you from moving forward.

Open your mind and your life up.

Day 166

Affirm this:

Today is a new day and a new opportunity
to accept my worth and who I am.

I am worthy of abundance, love, happiness, joy, and peace every day.

I am worthy, and the universe is manifesting this into my life.

I am accepting all that I receive from the universe today.

I am desiring an amazing life and path, and I
am worthy of all of this in my life.

I am truly blessed today by the universe and all my spirit
guides that are with me on my path, protecting me, leading
me, guiding me, and showing me a way to it all.

I appreciate my life, today and every day, as
I move forward into the best path.

Thank you, universe, for the love you
give me every day of my life.

Day 167

Let's transform so we can transform the world.

It needs change, and it is changing.

The world is in upheaval because it needs to change.

Just as this happens to us, it happens to the world as well.

Transformation is coming.

The world is transforming and shifting right now for us.

We are transforming and shifting with it.

We can shine brighter in the world for everyone to see.

We are in the midst of the transforming into love.

So, are you ready for it?

Day 168

Nobody is like you.

You are designed by you.

You are a unique individual from everyone else.

You try to fit in with the crowd so that you don't stand out.

But we are all different.

We all have different talents, gifts, knowledge,
and personalities, that are truly our own.

Stop hiding them.

Start being authentic and true to you.

Don't be ashamed of who you are.

You are a gift to the universe.

Show off who you are.

It's time to be different from the crowd, and follow a new,
unique path that is made for you and you only.

Your personality is your own.

Show it off.

You designed it.

Start to love who you are every day.

Day 169

Love all the things that make you strong.

Confidence. Love it.

Compassion. Love it.

Strength. Love it.

Love. Love it.

You. Love it.

Love yourself and all your strengths, and they will make your weaknesses stronger.

You get stronger the more you love yourself.

Be kind.

Be compassionate.

Be gentle.

It will help you heal and become stronger.

Love you.

Heal you.

Day 170

You deserve happiness in your life.

That is your true nature.

Start accepting that you can be happy,

Start choosing to be happy.

Happiness is born in your soul.

It's part of your DNA.

You let your ego take your happiness away when you listen to that voice in your head telling you that you don't deserve it.

You do.

Today choose to be happy.

Today start your day off with happiness inside your heart.

It's there waiting for you to choose it.

That's where God is waiting for you as well.

God is inside of you, waiting for you to see your true happiness and to spread it around on your path.

Start being happy.

That's where life is.

Day 171

When you start to choose yourself over another
that is hurting you, you start to heal.

Your love starts to turn inwards finally.

You have been so drained of energy trying to love, fix, help, support,
and lead others that you have forgotten to give those things to yourself.

You are running on empty.

You're done.

Giving love to yourself is as important as breathing.

Choosing you changes your life.

The universe literally shifts the world for you
when you shift your energy to yourself.

Start healing and choosing to love yourself every day.

Start filling yourself up again.

It's time for you.

Day 172

When you are seeking to heal, you need to let go of
the past and of the expectations of the future.

You have to forgive yourself, others, and stop being
attached to the should haves and could haves.

You need to stop feeling like you are still living there.

Dwelling on the past only hurts you now.

And your past is not in the now.

Looking at the past and the bad experiences only hurts you.

No one else.

Holding grudges only hurts you.

No one else.

Being angry and living in hate only hurts you.

No one else.

Part of healing is recognizing and being aware of these things inside
of you, then taking ownership of your emotions, feelings, senses,
thoughts, and actions, looking at them lovingly and gently.

Don't blame others for your own behaviour, words, actions, etc.

They are yours, not others.

Acceptance and forgiveness of all parties, including
yourself, is the important first step of healing.

Self-care, self-love, self-awareness, and awareness
of others are keys to healing.

These can be the biggest parts of healing that you don't want to face.

You don't like to think that you may have hurt
someone or that a loved one could hurt you.

But we are all humans, having experiences on this planet.

We all have egos that get in the way of being kind,
loving, compassionate, positive people.

Our egos hurt us and others.

We don't need to be ashamed or hold on to guilt, anger, or hate.

So, let it all go so you can start the healing process.

Let it all go so new energy will flow to you.

Once you realize this your world will shift.

The universe will shift for you and with you.

You have to make room for a new, higher
vibration and energy to come to you.

Healing energy.

Healing energy will flow when you make the intention to change.

Start your day off with appreciation, gratitude, and love.

Love heals; it is true and real.

Love cancels thoughts and feelings that are negative and hurtful.

Love is the truth of who you are, and it heals all wounds.

Healing is from a place of unconditional love for yourself.

Love yourself.

Heal yourself.

That's your power.

Day 173

Ease and flow in life is the place to live.

No attachments to an outcome.

Stop trying to predict how things should be.

That's a false belief.

You don't know.

God has more in store for you than you can even imagine.

And when you are ready, God will put those things in your path.

Divine timing is worth waiting for.

Patience and appreciating what you have prepare
you for the higher path to come.

It is coming to you.

Be ready.

It's on its way.

Day 174

Believe in yourself.

Don't wait for others.

You have to.

You can do this.

You've got this.

You are amazing.

You are beautiful.

You are awesome.

Make today about you and how you feel about you.

Believe in yourself today.

Day 175

We all have a destiny.

God controls the path to our destiny.

We have free will to choose how we get there
and how we react when we do.

If we get too far off-track, God and our spirit guides
put roadblocks and detours on our path for us.

Gently at first.

Then firmer if we do not hear the first one.

We can listen to the egoic mind and the negative,
toxic thoughts that led us down on every path.

Or we can choose to listen to God's way.

Then life is easier, more abundant, and full of love and life.

That is the best path to our destiny.

That is pure alignment with our dharma.

That's living the life of love.

It is also the path to awakening to our true, higher self.

The path home to God.

That is our destiny.

Day 176

Your mindset and focus can literally change everything in your life.

Your health, well-being, abundance, happiness, etc.

It's all determined by your mindset and focus.

It's truly transformational once you start to see it.

Start choosing to change your mindset and focus every day.

When you change your life, you will change the people around you as well as you start to light up your own path with love for yourself.

Choosing love, peace, and happiness over fear, hate, and anger, always makes for a better life.

Your mental health will change.

Depression, anxiety, worry, and fear will leave your path when you start to choose who you truly are.

Unconditional love, peace, happiness, joy, bliss, and anything positive is who you truly are at your core.

Start living your true self and changing your life for you.

The ones around you will also be affected by your darkness changing to light.

Always feel happy and blessed.

Always see the good, the reason, the purpose, and the lesson in every person and situation that you come along on your path.

Start shifting into your true self that is at your core.

Day 177

Many people want something else to make them
happy: a new house, spouse, job, car, life, etc.

That's all great if you are not trying to escape from your problems.

If you are trying to escape, the problems will just
follow you to the new circumstances.

The new situations won't change your life if you don't change yourself.

All your old problems will follow you if you don't
learn to change who you are on the inside first.

You bring you wherever you go.

You are the problem, unfortunately.

The solution is within, not in people, places, or things.

Change who you are, heal, then get the new life.

It always starts with you.

$\mathcal{D}ay$ 178

The power is within you to change your life.

To change yourself.

To envision yourself as the best version of you.

What is that for you?

What does it look and feel like to you?

Imagine if you could step into that dream
you have of being the best you?

You can.

Focus on it.

Envision it.

Don't have a doubt that it will unfold with every step you take forward.

To do this you have to let go of the old version of you.

The version that you have created up until now is
based on the vision you have had of yourself.

You created yourself with thoughts of how you speak to yourself, treat
yourself, and make choices and decisions in your life and on your path.

You are your own creation.

Create a great life for yourself by envisioning
what you want for yourself.

Feel it.

Be it.

You have that power.

That's how powerful you are in the universe.

You are a creator.

Start creating a better life and a better path
for yourself as you move forward.

Don't look back.

Make better choices and take better care of
your body and your mindset.

It's all yours to step into right now.

You are not just living life; you are creating it.

Day 179

You are lonely because you are not putting love into yourself.

Stop looking outside of yourself.

Staying busy is also toxic.

It distracts you from your true feelings.

You need to let go and let in the truth of who you are.

Instead of keeping busy, stop and sit in meditation, feeling the peace and love that come from being in the present moment.

Go from being someone to being no one in the present moment.

Have no identity in the present moment.

Be nothing in the present moment.

Just be.

When you sit in the nothingness, you will feel the real you.

This is an important step to self-love and self- care.

Meditation changes your life.

Meditating lets you feel who you truly are.

With daily practice it fills the void of loneliness with love, peace, and happiness as you go within and feel the love of God's energy flowing in you.

Start to meditate, love the true you, and live in love and peace.

Day 180

We cannot be loved unconditionally if we
don't know how to love ourself.

We don't even know how to receive that kind of love.

We don't even know what that kind of love feels like.

We cannot receive love fully either without
having unconditional love for ourself.

It truly is the most important part of our life.

Love.

We are love.

We are made of love.

Receiving love is harder if we don't love ourself.

We cannot heal without love for ourself.

We cannot change, grow, or evolve without love for ourself.

It's a priority and a universal truth for us.

Love is the only thing we need in our life to
grow and to change and to be more.

We are love, and we need to feel love for
ourself in order to live our best life.

Day 181

When things are not working in your life, you
need to let them go for a while.

Give them a rest.

There are things in your life that are working, though.

Do those things.

Stop looking at the things that are not
working in your life at the moment.

Let them go for now.

Focus on the things that are working in your life.

When you let go of the things that are not working and focus
on the things that are. you release the resistance on that path.

You allow things to flow because you have stopped
focussing on the things that aren't working.

You are now focussed on other things, and you allow the energy to
flow freely again to the problem to bring you the solutions you need.

You let the solutions in when you focus your attention somewhere else.

When you focus on the problem, you get more problems.

When you focus on the things that are flowing well, the
energy that came from your problems will stop flowing
to your path, and you can let the solutions in.

Resistance stops the flow.

It cuts it off.

Focus on the happy and good things that are going well.

Let that energy flow freely so that you can see, hear, and know the solutions that will come when you are resistant-free on your path.

Your energy goes where you focus.

Focussing on the good lets the energy flow freely into your life.

Let go of your problems.

They are getting in the way of the solutions.

True Love

This is my favourite bench.

I sit at this bench for inspiration, for peace, for contemplation, and for meditation.

This bench represents me and a future partner sitting on it and being in love with each other.

One day that person will be sitting with me, enjoying the view and each other's company.

This painting is about love and being in love.

Day 182

The universe shows you your journey every moment of the day.

Take time to stop and be still and to receive
the messages that itis giving you.

The universe is guiding you on this beautiful journey.

Let it steer you to the exciting path that you
are seeking and wanting to explore.

Itis whispering in your ear the way to go.

Make sure you are listening to it every day.

Day 183

Make your intent to stay awake and aware every day.

To live consciously.

Make it a choice as soon as you awaken in the morning.

It is how to start your day every day.

Ask God for clarity, guidance, and help with it.

God is in you to guide you through every day and
to awaken you to the truth of who you are.

Soon it will be an everyday way of life for you.

Day 184

Meditation is one of the most powerful and important
tools you can use in your life every day.

It silences the egoic mind and helps you to align with the love
that is flowing to you from the universe, God, source energy.

In meditation with a quiet mind, you just are.

This is your true state of being, just to be.

There are no labels, no preferences, no judgement,
and no likes or dislikes in this state of being.

That is who you truly are.

Just a soul in the moment, being aware of the moment.

In the moment of just being, you are awareness and consciousness.

That is who you truly are.

Awareness and consciousness.

A soul aware that you are in this vessel that helps you to create, learn,
and experience life through the eyes of God, here in this universe.

You are awareness.

Meditation helps you to connect to who you truly are.

This is why meditation, and a quiet mind are so important.

It also lets you hear the words, feelings, and sensations,
of our spirit guides, angels, masters, Jesus, and God
who want to communicate with you.

You can now align with that and hear, feel, see, know, and
follow the guidance instead of the false voice of your ego.

Meditate for at least thirty minutes or longer every day.

Don't stop because you don't feel or hear
anything; it takes time to get there.

It takes time to develop meditation skills and to get rid of
conditions that you have built up over all your lifetimes.

It will change your life over time, and you
will feel and see the difference.

Meditation is something you need to start doing every day.

Meditation changes your life.

Day 185

Affirm this:

Thank you for blessing me on this beautiful day.

My life is blessed, and I am loved every day.

I feel love and blessings flowing to me and
pouring into my path everywhere I go.

I love who I am, what I am doing, and where I am going.

I am guided, supported, and never alone on my journey.

God's energy is flowing with me as I go about my
day, living and breathing through me as one.

Today I have only love to give, only happiness to
spread, and only kindness in my heart.

Today I love myself in all that I do, and I
will lead with love as God does.

I am aligned on the path that leads back home to the creator.

God's energy is my home.

Thank you for this magnificent day
that is unfolding in front of me.

Day 186

Being true to yourself, your life, your path, and
your purpose is what you are here for.

It is so important to show up for yourself, stand
up for yourself, and believe in yourself.

It shows the universe that you show up for you, and the universe
will in turn give you more of what you are needing on your path.

If you are putting your energy into something that isn't for you,
you are wasting and draining it on something not meant for you.

Your path is your path and no one else's.

Stay true to it.

Don't let something veer you off your authentic path.

If you are genuine, your path will open up to more of that for you.

Day 187

Do you know how amazing you are?

You are amazing.

You get up and live your life in the best way you can.

You help others around you.

You show other people that you care and that you love them.

You treat others how you would like to be treated.

You create a path that you love and a life that you love.

Don't forget that you are doing a great job at everything you do.

Don't forget that you put your best foot forward always.

You show up for others.

You show up for you.

You are beautiful inside and out.

You are amazing, and don't ever think that you are not.

You are positive and full of life and love.

You are passionate and full of energy to walk your path today.

Show everyone how to be their best self every day.

Lead your life the way you want to.

You are amazing, you are beautiful, and you are you.

Don't forget that as you live your life today.

You are amazing today and every day.

Day 188

Loving yourself is truly how you heal.

It is the key to healing and changing your life for the better.

If you want to change, you have to do the work.

Loving yourself first is where you start.

You need to spread this message so others can heal and change as well.

You need to start knowing the truth and showing
others as you heal along the way.

Do you want to know why this is so important?

Because you are loved by your creator.

Everyone is loved equally by the creator.

That energy of unconditional love flows though everyone continuously.

And when you are out of alignment with that energy that
created you, you don't feel the love that is flowing to you.

You block it with other emotions that are out of alignment
with the pure, positive, loving energy that is flowing to you.

Loving yourself unconditionally is the key to pure
alignment with God's energy that created you.

So, start to love yourself by letting go of
anything that isn't aligned with love.

Being out of alignment only hurts you, so forgive and
let go of anything that doesn't serve your purpose, that
hurts you, that weighs you down, and triggers you.

Let go of it so that you can let the love you
deserve into you and onto your path.

You are deserving of this love, and you are worthy of it.

Love yourself every day so that you can live
your best and true life every day.

Day 189

Keep moving forward.

The things you left behind need to stay there.

The past is what helps you to change and grow
and be on a new and better path.

That's what the past does for us.

Always.

A learning experience.

A transforming experience.

The past can't hurt you anymore.

It changed you.

It helped you.

It made you stronger.

It gave you a new perspective and a new way of being.

Start looking at the positive things the past has done for you.

There are so many positive, life-changing moments in your past.

We think your past has hurt you, but really it
has changed you into a new person.

It evolved you.

It helped you.

Let go of past hurts.

They are no longer holding you; you are holding
them, and they are dragging you down.

That's heavy.

Let go of them.

Be free to see the good things your past brought to you because those things are freeing you and letting you soar higher and higher.

Day 190

When you are in survival mode and not happy with your life, you are living in fear of not having enough.

And you attract more of that into your life.

You attract what you are focussing on.

If you switch your mindset to appreciation, love, happiness, acceptance, and abundance, you will receive more of that into your life.

This will change and raise your vibration.

It will change you from fear to love.

When you live out of love, which is the vibration of enough, you are abundant.

And you attract more of that.

So, if you are always searching for money, you will always feel broke because of your mindset.

Switching your mindset changes your life.

Switching your mindset changes your reality.

Focus on abundance and appreciate all that you have and all that you are.

Love makes the world literally go around.

Day 191

Stop worrying about what could happen and
start thinking about what can happen.

Your life can be better.

Your life can be amazing.

Your life can be beautiful.

It will be once you let go of the fear that is holding you back.

Fear doesn't let the good in.

Fear blocks it.

Fear doesn't let your path flourish.

Fear doesn't let your mind grow.

Fear blocks everything good from flowing in.

Only when you start living your life out of love and
happiness will it start to grow and change.

Let go of your fear and live your life today.

Day 192

Every day you can choose to be the best you can,
or you can choose to stay the same.

If you choose to stay the same, stuck and toxic, you will live
in the pain of the past, the worry of the future, and you will
stay in the same patterns that are causing you more pain.

If you choose to be the best versions of yourself today and
every day, your life will change, grow, and become better.

You will love, and you will have peace and happiness.

But you have to make the choice to change.

If you stay in your comfort zone, you will stay small, and
you will live in fear and worry in your egoic mind.

Your life will never move forward if you stay in your comfort zone.

You have so much more to live for than that.

If you choose to step out of that box and leave your comfort zone, you
will start to bud and grow into something beautiful and magnificent.

You will take accountability for your life and your path.

You will take accountability for your behaviours and toxic patterns.

You will practice self-care, self-love, self-respect,
and you will take charge of your life.

You will start to see what you need to stop doing and who and what
you need to let go of that is holding you back from moving forward.

You will face the fears that your ego is instilling in you that are untrue.

You will start to have faith in your path and your life.

You will begin to love who you are and what
you have in your life and on your path.

Life can be amazing if you step up and out of your fear of change.

It's not that scary; it's transforming and beautiful.

So, embrace and love yourself, feel the change of newness coming, and don't be afraid of yourself.

Life change is beautiful.

Let it flow, let it happen, and let the rest go.

It's time to live a better life today.

Day 193

If you are living in fear today, you cannot live in love today.

Fear is the opposite of love.

You can't be both.

Living in love is who you truly are.

Living in fear is living untrue to yourself.

You are living in your false self, your ego.

Fear isn't who you are.

Love is.

You are made of love; unconditional love to be exact.

Fear is your ego.

You are innately made of pure love, energy,
light, happiness, peace, bliss, and joy.

This is who you truly are.

This is what we are all made of and who we all truly are.

Anything other than pure love is false.

It is fear.

You can't be in love if you hate.

You can't be in love if you are sad.

You can't be in love if you are worried.

You can't be in love if you spread gossip and lies.

You can't be in love if you hold grudges and dislike toward others.

You can't be in love if you are living in chaos.

There is nothing like love.

It's the energy of people, the planet, the universe,
God, animals, plants, and of nature.

Fear is an illusion that you need to let go of so that you
can start living your true path, true life, and true self.

Day 194

Your purpose is not to change the world.

Your purpose is to change yourself.

Your purpose is to create your own world that you love.

That's your purpose.

To be love and to spread it to others and to
help others feel that love inside.

You are creating your life with God, together.

God is never depressed, or angry, or suffering.

If you are in a negative mindset, you won't be able to feel God's energy.

God never wavers from the energy of love.

Start loving your life, your path, who you are, and where you are going.

Start doing the things you love to do every day.

You will then align with God and create an amazing, loving
life of abundance, peace, joy, love, and happiness.

That's your only purpose.

Day 195

You take our energy wherever you go.

You spread it around to whoever you meet.

Your energy is all over your path, your work,
in your home, and with your family.

Your energy is transferred to others.

It flows all around you for everyone to feel.

Spread the energy of unconditional love
on your path, wherever you go.

Your energy is like a signature, unique, and
you attract or repel with your energy.

If it's negative, you will attract more negative
energy and people on your path.

If it's positive, you will attract more positive
energy and people on your path.

You will repel negative energy if you are positive.

You will repel positive energy if you are negative.

It's important to raise your vibration to a positive
energy in order to change your path and life.

Stop being negative, full of hate and anger, carrying
grudges, living in the past, and having toxic habits.

It does nothing but add fuel and momentum to the fire.

This is a direct reflection of your energy.

If it's negative, you need to change yourself and heal,
then be a part of the change in this world.

You need to raise your vibration out of the negative
flow of energy and into the positive.

Everyone plays a role in this universe, and your part is to
raise our vibration to the positive and flow it to others.

Changing this world starts with you, and it will
affect you so much on your path.

It will change your life today.

Day 196

Life really is in the moment.

You have nothing going wrong.

Everything is moving forward.

You are healing in this moment.

You are growing, changing, and evolving in this moment.

There is nothing going wrong.

It's all unfolding and happening as it should.

It's a process.

There is no end game.

You are moving forward and getting there day by day.

Day 197

It's truly a blessing to wake up and smile and say you love this day.

It's a blessing from God to see that your life is
amazing and unfolding as it should.

There is no right way or right path.

There is only your path.

There is only your own unique path that you are being led down.

It's unfolding as you go.

It's unfolding as you make your choices in the day.

It's your path, it is what you make of it.

It's a blessing for you and you only.

Your path is beautiful, if you see it that way.

Your path is hard, if you see it that way.

It's all about your view of your path and life.

What are you viewing on your path?

The beauty of it or the challenge of it?

Viewing the beauty make the challenges softer and easier.

Viewing the challenges only blinds you from the beauty,
and you will only see the challenges on your path.

Shift your view, your perspective, and your mindset today,
and you will see your path and life change significantly.

See your path light up differently by changing your view.

$\mathcal{D}ay$ 198

Are you pretending to be someone you're not?

Are you trying to fit into someone else's box or path to please them?

Are you aware that this is making you small?

It's making you miss out on the life that you want and
that you decided to create before you came here.

You have your own unique path to walk, and it leads to
your own purposes, gifts, lessons, talents, soul mates and
soul tribes, and passions that are specifically for you.

You have your own life.

Stop trying to fit into someone else's that is clearly not meant for you.

If you feel out of place, like you don't fit into the puzzle that
is in front of you, it's because you are not meant to.

You are meant to make your own way, and you will fit perfectly.

When you start living your life for you, not for everyone else.

It's exhausting trying to be someone you are not.

It's exhausting to try and fit in where you are not supposed to.

That's work and resistance telling you to find a new way.

Your own way.

Your own unique way.

Step off, out, and into your own world, universe, and path
that you create with your own unique, individual mind.

The pieces to your puzzle will fall together easily, and
it will make a picture that you need to see.

The people that are meant for you will fit in,
and you will feel at home with them.

Attract your path by always being you.

Don't keep trying to fit in where you don't belong.

You have a place on your own path that's within you, waiting to
unfold when you are true to who you are and where you want to go.

$\mathcal{D}ay$ 199

Affirm this:

Thank you, angels and guides, God and my spiritual team.

I am truly blessed every day with the guidance, help,
and inspiration that I receive from you.

You are with me through thick and thin.

You are with me when I may forget that you are with me.

You never forget me or leave me.

You are with me when I have lost my way, and
you always bring me back on track.

You are with me when I have lost my faith in
myself, and you always have faith in me.

You always have the answer I need when I am searching for one.

I am truly blessed to have such support, guidance, and help on my path.

My team is amazing and know me so well.

Thank you for being with me today and every day to show me the
way to my purpose, my path, my passions, and all that I love.

I love you all so much unconditionally, and I know
I am loved back with enormous love.

It's a beautiful feeling to know I am never alone, and I never will be.

It's a beautiful feeling to know that love is with me every day.

Thank you for being by my side.

I ask you to help me today, to guide me today,
and to show me the way today.

You are appreciated by me so much today and every day.

Day 200

Let your heart calm and your mind quiet.

Feel the present moment.

Relax into the universe, and let it hold you in the moment.

Let yourself float.

Let yourself be free.

Serenity is around you in every moment.

Close your eyes and be free from your
stresses, even if only for a moment.

Your soul will appreciate it, and you will appreciate
the feel of serenity around you.

Even if it is only for a moment.

Day 201

Hard times are a lesson on your path.

It is time to change and grow.

Find the gift in it.

Whatever is happening is because there is
something more coming for you.

Something manifesting that you can't even imagine.

Things all happen for a reason.

To let go means you can let in the new that is coming to you.

Don't get discouraged.

Your path will be different but truly amazing.

Don't be afraid of change.

Change means transformation, growth, learning, and evolving.

There is more to come for you, my friend.

Get up and live.

Day 202

When you exchange a smile or conversation with another,
you are flowing your energy to that person.

You are sending them love as well.

You also never know what your words can do for another.

A simple act of kindness can change a person's day.

They won't forget you.

You can also plant a seed in a person with a simple conversation.

There is so much this small act can do for people.

When you give, you receive.

Giving is receiving.

Speak to everyone you pass on a walk, in a store, or anywhere you go.

Words are powerful.

They change you.

They can change others.

Kindness can change everyone around you.

Choose to be kind to everyone you meet, no matter
who they are or what they are doing.

This could be you at any given moment.

This small act is like a ripple.

It affects so many, and you don't even know it.

Day 203

You don't have to go anywhere to love God.

You are one with God everywhere you go.

You are connected to God everywhere you go.

God is in you in each moment of every day.

You don't have to go anywhere except inside yourself to love God.

God's love is flowing to you everywhere.

It's in you to feel, and it's in you to give.

Know that you can love God in all the places you go.

God is always guiding you, supporting you, helping
you, loving you, and showing you the way.

You are partners with God, and you are together
on this beautiful path that you walk along.

God's love is always there for you.

Align with God's love.

See it; know it; feel it; be it.

Day 204

Affirm this:

Today is the start of a new day.

The start of a new me.

Every day I am a better version of me.

My intentions today are to be me on my path.

To be my truest self that I know today.

To let go of the old ways and old patterns that
stop me from being that better person.

To choose a healthy mindset and lifestyle and a better me every day.

Today is always for me.

Today I love me.

Today I am stepping into something beautiful and
amazing because I am beautiful and amazing.

Today I choose to love me.

Day 205

We walk almost every day.

It's important to be outside and to connect
with the natural world around us.

We are connected to nature, and it is connected to us.

It helps us to get out of depression and anxiety
as we see the beauty around us.

It's everywhere.

This puts us in the present moment.

Where life is.

Nature is God's creation for us to see, and so He can
feel and see His creation from our point of view.

We are one with everything.

Walking does so much for us.

It helps our mental health; it can be a time of
meditation; it helps keep us healthy and fit.

Walking uplifts, us and changes our mood.

Get out and walk on your path and absorb
the beauty everywhere around you.

Thank God for the beautiful view.

Day 206

Stop seeking validation and love from others.

Those people are not responsible for you.

You are responsible for you and you only.

You don't need love from others.

You need love from you.

You have love from God.

Love from the inside out.

Not from the outside in.

You are made of love.

Love is in you always to give to yourself.

Show up for yourself, and give yourself that love that is in you.

It's yours.

You are blocking it by seeking love outwardly.

It's not there.

It's not in others.

It's in you.

It's in the connection between you and God only.

Feel that love radiating and flowing to you
freely from the energy of God.

It's there for you to receive.

It's yours. and it's flowing freely to you every moment of your life.

That love will change your life; it will change your path, and it will change who you are.

Love yourself first.

Day 207

Step into the power that you have inside of you.

Step out of the fear of your ego and into the light and love of God.

We all have inner power, of intuition and guidance
from the higher sources of the universe.

Don't be afraid to listen to your heart and feel the love that
God is pouring into you and showing you every day.

To step into this power God says you need to love yourself first,
as He loves you unconditionally in every moment of your life.

You are here for the love and energy, and you
are here to be guided by that love.

God wants us to become our truest self and to show that to the world.

Stop living small, and stop being afraid of your inner power.

It's there for you as a gift from God to change your life,
the ones around you, and the world as you know it.

Show love to yourself and to everyone you meet.

Believe, know, and step into that love.

Believe in yourself.

Finding self-discipline, self-love, self-respect, and self-worth can be the hardest part of moving forward.

Choosing to be better every day is more difficult than choosing to keep living as you are, stuck, unhappy, and angry.

Making a new routine, choosing a new habit, and finding a new way of thinking can be challenging at first.

Stopping a bad habit or addiction and choosing to do something else instead of the toxic choice can be difficult.

You have to be aware of the choices you make in your life every day.

Your choices determine where you are going and who you will be as a soul.

Self-discipline is in your control.

It's up to you to make better choices to change and to be a better version of you.

It takes sixty-six days to let go of a habit or add a new one to your routine, but it will take longer if you don't have self-discipline, self-love, self-respect, and self-worth in your life every day.

Respect, love, and know yourself.

Be your true self.

Stop listening to your ego.

It's keeping you in that negative mindset, forcing you to stay small and in your comfort zone.

Change your bad habits, choices, and ways, and choose you instead.

It's up to you, no one else, to do the work to change your life.

You have to have self-discipline to keep changing and moving forward into something so beautiful you can't even imagine it.

Let your beautiful soul show by being true to you who you really are.

Day 209

Affirm this:

Today is a day of faith and trust.

Today I awaken and have faith in the life in front of me.

My path will unfold just as it's supposed to.

My path is divine and blessed.

I know that everyone is connected divinely by the source of God.

I know that my path flows with divinity and love.

Today I trust in that flow of love and have faith that the divine energy I trust in will show me the next step when I get there.

I don't have to have fear on my path.

Because there is so much love for me in the here and the now.

I don't have to worry on my path.

I don't have to know what's ahead on my path because I trust that the divine is leading me and holding my hand on it today and every day.

We are all divinely led.

We are all divinely loved.

We are all divinely blessed.

We are all divine.

Today I trust that my path is perfect, beautiful, and unfolding as God planned.

Today I trust and surrender to the now and merge with the divine guidance that we are all connected to.

I know that we are all divine, and we are all loved.

Day 210

You have to open up your mind to new ideas and new paths.

If you keep staying the same you will never change, grow, or evolve.

Being teachable means opening your mind to new
opportunities, new paths, and new perspectives.

If you keep thinking the same, you will always stay in
your comfort zone, not moving forward in life.

Your comfort zone is keeping you small and afraid of moving forward.

Your comfort zone is teaching you that there is
nothing more for you on your path.

There is so much for you outside of that small box you are in.

There is life.

That's where your purpose, your passions, and your
life is, outside of that comfort zone you are in.

Break it open, and learn something new.

See something new.

Be someone new.

Become alive, loving your life on a deeper level.

If someone is showing up that is outside your box, go with them.

Let them show you a new way of being,
living, and loving your life again.

Break open the box.

Day 211

Sunrises and sunsets are magnificent.

They are a show just for us.

This is God showing us the true beauty of our planet.

Of our universe.

We are all connected to the universe by energy.

God's energy and the sun's energy.

This show of a sunrise or sunset makes us stop and appreciate
the energy that is being given to us every moment of the day.

The sun is the most important star in our galaxy.

It gives us energy, light, and heat.

It gives us life.

We are a part of the sun.

We absorb its energy in everything we consume.

It asks nothing in return and keeps giving and giving to us.

Without the sun, our world and galaxy wouldn't exist.

So, the next time you see a sunrise or a sunset,
give appreciation to it for giving life.

Day 212

May your heart be full of love and joy today as you celebrate
what you have and what you appreciate in life.

Appreciate your family, your friends, your home,
your job, and the food that you eat today.

You are blessed; you are loved; you are embraced by the energy of love.

When you appreciate all you have on your path
and in your life, you receive more.

Celebrate your life.

Celebrate where your life is taking you every day.

Cherish the moments you have with everyone
you meet moving forward.

Today is a day for happiness, joy, love, appreciation, and abundance.

Let go of anything that isn't that feeling of love.

Let the love of life into your heart.

You are blessed.

You are loved.

You are beautiful.

The Tree of Colour

I truly love trees.

They are beautiful to me.

They are the most amazing species that the universe
has provided us with on this planet.

If it wasn't for trees, we would not be here on this beautiful earth.

They provide us with oxygen, food, shelter, wood to build
things and to keep us warm, and the list goes on.

They are beautiful, and they are my favourite thing to paint.

This piece of artwork reflects the love I have
for trees, the earth, and for colour.

TOBrien

Day 213

Self-love helps you to build up your self-esteem, self-worth, and self-respect.

Love does so much for you.

It changes your life.

If you put effort into you instead of putting yourself down, you would be on top of the world instead of hating yourself.

What brought you to the lowest point on your path?

What made you stop loving yourself?

Other people?

Their words about you can hurt, but they are not the truth.

They don't know you.

They don't even know the truth of who they are themselves, yet you allow them to control how you feel and tell you who you are.

Stop giving your power away to others.

Stop putting your happiness and love in the hands of others because they don't even know what to do with their own happiness and love.

Ignore others' words that are negative, unkind, and hurtful.

They are struggling too with loving themselves.

They hurt others because they don't know how to feel the love that is truly inside of them.

If someone is putting you down, know that these words are not the truth.

Leave.

Don't stay.

Walk away.

Know your truth and know your worth.

You are made of pure energy, love, joy, bliss, happiness, and peace.

We all are.

Anything else is a lie.

Believe in yourself, and love yourself,

Step into the power that is yours.

Don't let anyone tell you differently because
they don't know who they are.

You do now.

You are divinely loved and blessed in your life and on your path.

Everyone is.

$\mathcal{Day}$ 214

Life isn't about what you have; it's about how you feel inside.

Life is the feeling of love inside.

Love is your life.

To have a great life, you have to have your heart on your path.

Your heart must be open to give and receive love on your path.

Love is the basis of everything in you and around you.

Life isn't about acquiring material things.

Life is about loving what's in your life already.

That's what makes you feel whole.

Loving who you are and what's inside you, that's what life is.

Life isn't outside of yourself.

Life is in your heart and soul.

Love is life, and life is love.

When you see what's on the inside of yourself, you will love everywhere you go and everything you have.

You don't need anything in your life but love for yourself.

God created you out of this love.

Day 215

Every thought we think is a prayer.

Words are energy.

Everything we speak sends out a vibration of what
we want, who we are, what we like and don't like,
where we want to go, and what we want to do.

So, if you want something that is lacking in your life, it
won't come if you are asking out of desperation.

Desperation is a negative vibration.

The universe knows vibrations.

So, your vibration is important when sending
out prayers or even just speaking.

Say your words to God's energy to match that vibration.

Out of love, abundance, appreciation, joy, and happiness.

That vibration matches God's energy, and you can manifest from there.

God's energy always gives you what you want, but
it's vibrating at that frequency of love.

Unconditional love.

Pray from love, appreciation for what you have, for
who you are, and for where you are going.

Match the love of the universe when you pray or ask for anything.

Love makes the world go around.

It's the frequency of your true and highest self.

Day 216

Affirm this:

Today is a day of letting go of what doesn't serve me.

Today is a day of letting go of the hurt that is holding me back in life.

Today is a day for letting in things that benefit my life.

I am letting unconditional love, peace, happiness, clarity, harmony, calmness, intuition, ease, and flow into my life.

I am letting go of hate, fear, chaos, confusion, anger, frustration, and resistance.

These are old traits holding me back.

I am letting go of everything that's stopping me from moving forward.

I am ready to change my life.

I am ready to change into something new.

I am ready to spread my wings and open up my heart to freedom, to love, and to connect with my soul, which has been calling me toward this my entire life.

I hear my soul calling my name today.

My soul is guiding me to my best life.

I want to live it.

Starting today I am new; I am free to be me.

Starting today I live for me and my purpose.

I love this life that the universe is giving me today.

Thank you for showing me the way!

Day 217

When you start to change, you will see a difference in yourself.

You will not be triggered by people or situations.

You will be able to pause and look at things and learn from them.

Change won't be as scary to you anymore.

You will embrace it because you will know it is
showing you a new way and a new perspective.

Healing will give you peace, calmness, joy, and happiness.

Most importantly, it will give you love in your heart again.

Healing will help you see a new path, a new life, and a new you.

You will love yourself; you will respect yourself;
you will know your worth and your truth.

No one will take that away from you again because you are aware of
toxicity and drama and chaos, and you will want no part of it anymore.

You will love peace.

You will have boundaries, communication, and
healthy relationships all around you.

You are growing, expanding your consciousness,
and evolving into your true self.

Don't stop.

It never ends.

Healing, learning, and growing will always be on your path, but they
will get easier and easier every day with the love you will give yourself.

Day 218

Life really is one day at a time.

If you got everything at once it wouldn't be enjoyable.

It's a journey on your path, and where it takes you is the thrill of life.

You honestly don't know where the twists
and turns are until they show up.

You have no control of the future.

You only have now.

You need to just enjoy the ride, no matter where it takes you.

You can go around and around if you choose to.

You can go backwards, but you shouldn't; life is forward facing.

You can just stay where you are, but life gets dull in the same spot.

You can wear the spot down if you sit too long.

Not moving forward is not living, it's suffering.

Live in the now.

Live each day to the fullest.

Life is in every day and nowhere else.

So, live your life in love, and keep walking
forward day by day into your life.

$\mathcal{Day}$ 219

The now is where reality is.

The now is where happiness is.

The now is where your true self is.

The now is the only spot to be.

Be in the now.

Let go.

Forgive, surrender, and have faith.

The now is where you are.

Day 220

The phrase "easier said than done" keeps you stuck.

Take this saying out of your vocabulary.

It keeps you in a negative mindset and vibration.

It makes things seem difficult and challenging.

No one said that healing was easy.

Stop thinking that.

You have to choose to do the work to heal.

You have to choose to be better.

And no, it isn't easy.

It's not supposed to be.

If you know that you need to heal and be a better
person, you will have an easier path to healing.

But no, it is not easy to start the path.

The mental work still needs to be faced, worked
through, and felt in order to change.

But once you know what to do, it gets easier as you go.

On the other side of change and growth,
there is a new you waiting for you.

A new life.

A new person.

A new beginning.

It gets easier as you go, and you learn to level up and evolve.

It gets easier once you choose to see that.

It gets easier when you see that you need to take that first uncomfortable step to start changing and healing.

Difficult situations don't have to be hard, but when you say, "easier said than done," you stop yourself from moving forward.

It keeps you stuck in fear of being new.

It blocks you from moving forward.

Start saying:

"This path will unfold once I make the intention to change and be better, one step at a time."

It gets easier and easier once you start taking the steps to change.

Day 221

Life is never done.

There is always more.

There is no end goal because that's never enough.

We desire more.

If we didn't, life would be boring.

Life never ends.

We are always learning, growing, evolving, and changing.

Even after our bodies are gone, we are in another realm,
doing the same thing on a different dimension.

Life is eternal and never-ending; there are no limits.

We are life.

Day 222

Don't be afraid today.

Don't be afraid to make mistakes.

Don't be afraid to do something new or something different.

Don't be afraid to step on a path that is unknown.

Don't be afraid to be who you are today.

Don't be afraid to speak your truth.

Don't be afraid to move forward.

You have to let go of your fear of life, of being
wrong, of making a mistake, of being hurt,

and of growth.

You need to start walking and living your truth.

There is no fear in the truth.

There is only love in the truth.

Fear stops you from growing, moving forward, changing, and evolving.

Fear is your ego, and you need to let go and see what fear truly is.

Fear is an illusion.

There is nothing to be afraid of.

Fear controls you, and you have to stop being controlled by
something that doesn't even know what the word love means or is.

Fear holds you back.

Love moves you forward.

Be in love with your life, with yourself, and with your path.

Stepping out of fear and into love changes your life.

It allows you to flow and move and to be you.

Don't let anything stop you today.

Fear is not real, and it is not who you are.

Day 223

My light shines bright today.

It shows me the way to love, peace, happiness, joy,
excitement, and to the love and light of God.

My light is showing me the way home.

It shines on my path for all things to see me
and to draw them into my light.

It shines so bright today.

My light is full of love and all that is good.

My light never dims.

It shines so bright today.

Like a moth to a flame, people are guided to my light.

I attract all who need to see and feel my light and love.

I shine brightly for you.

Your light will ignite brighter in my light.

Your light will spark and grow into a flame.

My light is your light because we are all the same.

Together we will find even more light on the path home to God.

We will light the path for others to see and
light the flame again inside of them.

Join my light.

My light is your light, and my light is for all to see.

My light shines brighter today as I connect to more light on my path.

My light is brighter today for all to see.

$\mathcal{D}ay$ 224

You are the master of your own life.

You have done this before in many different lifetimes.

To become a master of life, you must practice
your skills over and over again.

To become a master of life, you must put your heart into it and
be passionate about your skills and where they are taking you.

You can master your life and your path by having
love, passion, and faith in yourself.

A master of life has no doubts that they can
do or be anything or anyone.

A master of life never wavers and knows that
life is unfolding how it should.

A master of life has patience to develop their skills
and makes time for them every day in their life.

A master of life knows the truth and how to use
that truth on their path and in their life.

You know how to master a skill; it's the same as mastering your life.

It takes daily practice, love, passion, patience,
and eagerness to get better and better.

It takes knowledge, will power, determination,
inspiration, and excitement to move forward in life,
with this energy of life that you are mastering.

Everyone is a master of their own life; they just have to
have the master mindset and the will to become one.

You are the master of your life, so start stepping into it and knowing it.

You are a master of life.

Day 225

Who is leading your life?

Is it your ego or your true self?

You can tell by the path that you are taking.

Is your path in chaos, or is it in peace?

Is your path in anger, resentment, and fear, or is it in laughter and love?

Is your path sad and lonely, or is it happy and abundant?

Take a look at your life.

Chaos, anger, resentment, fear, hate, judgement, lack, guilt, shame, sadness, and anything else that is negative and bringing you down is your ego leading your life.

This is what living in your ego does for you.

It robs you of joy, happiness, peace, bliss, abundance, love, and anything positive in your life.

Your ego wants you to be small and in fear.

Your ego lives in fear and does not know

what love is, so it's not aware of what or

who your true self is.

It has no awareness.

Love is your true self.

The ego is your false self.

Who is leading your life?

Day 226

Are you a complainer or someone who appreciates?

Do you talk about the things you are lacking in your
life, or do you appreciate what you have?

Are you focussing on the bad things about yourself, others,
your life, and your path, or are you focussing on the good?

Take control today of what you are focussing on being and doing.

Be aware of your thought and change them to good ones.

Your reality is what you think and believe.

Your thoughts truly turn into your reality.

Don't believe the bad thoughts; look around,
reflect on your life, and what is in it.

Do stress, frustration, no money, depression, bad luck,
jealousy, toxic people, etc., seem familiar to you?

Or do happiness, love, abundance, joy, bliss, freedom,
ease and flow, calmness, and peace?

What are you focussing on to make your life better?

Stop complaining and start appreciating and
watch your reality change for the better.

Day 227

Surrender.

Let everything go that you think is.

Because it is not what you think.

You can't even imagine what the universe has for you.

Let go of the idea that you know.

Surrender to the unknown.

Let things happen the way they are supposed to unfold.

That's surrendering.

Day 228

Helping others is our purpose.

To impact others' lives.

To help others see the way.

To be of service to the universe.

To be living kindly, generously, compassionately, and peacefully with others in this universe and on our path.

This is who we are, and this is what we should be doing.

Spreading love, kindness, and joy to everyone we meet.

This is what we are here for, and this is who we are truly.

Day 229

If something is not working, then let it go.

Stop focussing and trying so hard.

If it is not working, then there is a reason.

Maybe it's not working because there are bigger
and better things coming for you.

Let it go.

Focussing on things that aren't working only adds resistance
and gives you more of what's not working on your path.

When you focus on what is working, you get more of that.

When you are focussing on the good that is working in your life, you
are letting go of the resistance of what isn't working in your life.

When you let go of resistance, you allow things to be aligned
so that the path that wasn't working can now come to you.

This is why it is important to stop trying so hard to make
things work or happen the way you think they should.

You get attached to certain outcomes and forget
that you can't control what happens.

Let things flow how they are going to flow.

Let things be as they are going to be without
trying to direct or control life.

Live in the flow of life.

Let it go; let life happen.

Let life be as its going to be.

Living in the flow is where life is.

Day 230

What you focus on in our life is what you get.

If you feel down, depressed, sad, angry, hurt, unworthy, resentful, jealous, etc., then that is your vibration to the universe and because of the law of attraction, the universe gives you more of that.

You have to start flipping your story.

Be worthy.

Be love.

Be happy.

Be positive.

Let go of the old pain.

Forgive others and yourself for the past.

It's gone and done.

Step into a different storyline.

It's time to start being a better book.

A better storyteller.

Start a new chapter.

Start living.

You deserve it.

Day 231

Affirm this:

Every day is the best day of my life.

Every day gets better and better.

As I go through each day, I ascend higher and higher.

I look forward to the next day every day because
I know it will be even better than today.

My love for my life grows and grows each day.

I am always connected with the source that makes
each day better and better for me.

Every day I learn more, know more, and change.

I love my life.

I love my path.

I love where it is leading me.

I step toward my true self, and I am living
my best life every step of the way.

Day 232

You can either choose to feel bad or to feel good.

It is your own choice, not others to change your life.

What are you choosing to see, do, or be in each moment?

It is all on you to make the right choices
that align with your higher self.

Start being aware of your choices.

Start living from awareness.

It changes your path, life, and you.

Day 234

When you start to make yourself and your
path a priority, your life changes.

When you start to love yourself, who you are, and
where you are, your life will start to change.

When you see the good inside yourself, on your path,
and in your life, your world starts to shift.

Putting yourself first isn't wrong.

It's a priority.

Letting go of behaviours and patterns that hold you back,
limit you, bring your well-being down, and that are toxic is
necessary to let in all the good that you want in your life.

It is important to create boundaries and keep them
in order to move forward in a healthy way.

It's time to say, "I love myself, and I don't
want to live this way any longer."

Choose yourself because only you can make that choice for you.

Day 235

Have a silly and fun day today.

Make others laugh today.

Make yourself laugh today.

The day goes by faster when you are happy.

Focus on the good.

Keep smiling.

Keep laughing.

Life is fun.

Enjoy it to the fullest.

Day 236

Joy is in all of us.

We are made from joy and love.

It's part of who we are truly.

Joy helps us see the good, the happiness that is in our life.

Joy opens our heart to love.

Joy helps us seek pleasure, passion, happiness, and love.

Embracing the feeling of joy moves us forward
into an amazing path of who we truly are.

Joy feels so good to us because we were born
with this beautiful trait inside of us.

Seeking joy keeps us on the path to home.

It's the way home.

So, keep following your joy, and see what exciting
experiences happen to you along the way.

Day 237

Let yourself be free today.

Surrender to your true self today.

Peace, love, and happiness; that is who you are.

Let go of that ego that makes you feel small.

Be you today.

Be authentic and be real.

Don't care what others think of you; their opinions are false.

Just be you today.

Be unique today.

Today is all you have.

Live for you today.

Day 238

How do you surrender?

How do you live in the flow of life?

You have to put your worries aside, your past aside, and your ego aside.

You have to be able to forgive, love, and open your heart to receive
the healing energy that God is flowing to you in a constant stream.

To surrender and heal you must let go, look within yourself,
stop blaming others, see and accept your mistakes and
those of others, and forgive yourself and others.

Ask God to help you on this path.

Asking is the key.

When you set an intention to heal, the universe
shifts to help you on your path to healing.

This path isn't easy, so don't give up.

You have the whole universe by your side,
supporting you and cheering you on.

Surrendering, trusting, having faith, and letting go will get
you moving forward to the next level, to a better you.

Day 239

Nothing can stop you.

You are living life every day, and the universe is guiding you to everything you ever wanted.

Let it in.

Stop worrying.

Be happy and see the blessings come pouring in.

The only thing stopping it is you.

You have to let go of the old and let in the new.

The old is blocking the way.

Let go.

Let in what you have been waiting for on your path.

Day 240

The time is now.

You need to change more than ever.

It's time to be your best self.

It's time to change your thoughts.

It's time to see who you really are.

It's time to be free of hurt.

It's time to be different.

It's time to be the real, true you.

Are you ready to step into your power?

Day 241

You really have to relax in life.

Be at peace.

Love what you are doing in the present moment.

Heal and live from your heart space.

Open your heart, and let it lead you to the next step and the next.

Do what you are inspired to do each day.

See the beauty in each day and in yourself and
appreciate whatever comes to you.

There is a lesson and a gift in each situation that comes to you.

Always a lesson.

God is with you every step of the way.

Have faith, relax, and let life flow to you every day.

Day 242

We are all in the world together.

We are all connected by the energy of love and God.

We have to support each other, love each other,
and be compassionate to each other.

Love is the only way to step into a new path and
become the true people we are meant to be.

Love is our power.

Love is our divinity.

Love is our true self.

Love is the path to oneness.

Love is the path to the truth.

Love will change us and the others around us.

We are all connected by the energy of love.

Unconditional love.

We are all here to feel this energy of God that flows
through us and in everything that is in the universe.

We are all connected by the energy of love.

Our true self is love, and we are full of it,

We need to show love to ourself, and feel it every day.

To choose to love instead of hate.

Love takes us everywhere.

Love gives us everything we need to walk the true path of life.

We need to live in the energy of love and the energy of God.

They are one and the same, flowing through us.

When we are in alignment, our life will transform.

Day 243

You keep looking for love in all the wrong places.

Love is not outside of you.

You are putting your happiness in other people's hands.

It's your responsibility to love yourself, to heal, and to
make choices that make you happy, not others.

God loves you unconditionally, with so much love.

It's so beautiful the amount of love that is flowing
to you through the energy of God.

Love is pouring to you from God all day.

You can't feel it because you are not aligned with your love for yourself.

Loving yourself and doing the things you love to do
allows you to feel that love pouring into you.

It starts with you and no one else.

Stop the pity party and start to love your life for you.

Start loving who you are, what you are doing, and where you are going.

Step into your power of light and love because it is in you to feel.

There is so much love for you here.

When you are out of alignment with love, putting life
and yourself down, and asking others to love you, you
are looking for love in all the wrong places.

Shine your light; it's yours to shine.

Day 244

Trying so hard is a problem in most people's lives.

Do you try and try to do something and get nowhere?

You have to stop trying and instead be aware.

There is a difference.

Awareness of the present moment takes us into the present moment.

Trying is something forced and its resistance.

Doing things like meditating, walking, a hobby, creating something, or listening to self-help videos or music can keep you living in the present.

Enjoying what you are doing in the moment, by letting go of the negativity, the dwelling in the past, and the looking to the future, is key to changing.

When you are doing things that you love or seeing the good and the beauty in every moment, that is where your life is.

That's presence.

If you feel yourself drifting from it, be aware and look around you at what is right there.

In that moment.

At what you are doing.

Being aware of your thoughts is important.

Awareness is the key to the present moment.

Life is hard when you are changing into someone new.

It's part of the journey, but so is love.

Loving yourself, your life, your path, and
the life force that is within you.

Seeing the love in your life pulls you to more of it.

It becomes easier and easier as you keep going.

Love and awareness are key to changing and
growing and transforming your life.

Lavender in a Bucket

This piece of artwork is so serene, so peaceful, and so inviting.

It is soft and easy.

You can almost smell the fragrance.

I love the smell of lavender; it is so calming and relaxing.

Can you smell it?

Inhale the fragrance; breathe it in.

This beautiful purple will help you to surrender.

T. O'Brien

It's Time to Believe in Yourself — 297

$\mathcal{D}ay$ 245

Affirm this:

I feel your love; I feel your guidance; I trust your guidance.

You are the way to everything beautiful, everything peaceful, and to unconditional love

in my life.

You give me strength when I don't have it.

You give me love when I don't feel it.

You give me direction when I am lost.

You give me words when I have no words to speak.

You give me faith that I am going the right way toward home and you.

I love my journey; I love my path; I love who I have become.

God is leading my life today and every day.

We are together on the road to light, love, peace, and happiness.

I am excited to see what's next on my path.

I look forward to that amazing light that I am stepping into on my path.

Thank you, God, for being in me, with me, and in my life.

Day 246

We walk a higher path.

We walk with a higher purpose.

We walk with a brighter light.

We are old souls.

We are here for you.

We are masters of life, awakening again to show you the way.

We are here for you.

We are old souls.

Stand in our light and shine too.

Day 247

To have a great relationship, any relationship, you
have to be happy and in love with yourself.

Truly happy and healed from past traumas
and in love with yourself wholly.

When you are whole, then you can love your
partner or friend and family the same.

Happiness is in you first.

When you have your own happiness, you will have
a beautiful relationship with another.

This is the key to a great, lasting relationship.

If you are not aligned with your love for yourself,
you will try to seek that from another.

Your happiness and love are not in them, it's in you.

If you're struggling with your relationship with anyone, reflect
and see where you are not showing up for yourself.

Your relationship with yourself is so important before
seeking a relationship with anyone else.

Love yourself truly and unconditionally,
then you can give that to others.

Day 248

Living life without expecting a certain outcome on your
path will make it easier to not be disappointed.

But you hope for things to come.

Because life just is as it is.

That's the problem.

So, you hope for things and when they don't
happen, you are disappointed every time.

Life is just as it is.

You don't know where your path is going to lead you.

Your life is unfolding as it should.

You never know what surprises or turns or
miracles the universe has in store for you.

Hope can help you stay positive, but it also has a fear vibration to it.

If you stand in hope, knowing that the universe has
your back and is leading you to where you need to go,
then that hope can turn into trust and faith.

You will accept the path that you are following,
and you will have trust in it.

There are no expectations, then.

You just follow and allow.

Life just is as it is.

You don't have to hope for anything anymore.

You allow things to be as they are and accept
the truth that life is offering you.

Day 249

You have to start believing in yourself and walk the higher road.

Just live and love your life and yourself.

Your life will start to transform, and you will become
a new person once you see all you have to do in
love to live your life and path authentically.

Live your life with your heart in the lead so
that others can follow your example.

Become a shower of life for others to follow your example.

Walk your path tall so that others will follow.

They will wonder how you are living your best life.

Soon you will be helping others to heal and move forward.

Just walk your path and love your life.

Be yourself.

Be your true self.

Be unique.

Be you always.

Day 250

Your day starts and ends with you.

If your day starts with appreciation, love for your life,
love for the day ahead, and happiness to be who you
are, you will change the path you are walking on.

You will walk at a higher level of consciousness.

If you choose to start your day off with love for yourself and
for what you have, you will bring more love into your life.

Your path will fill up with things you love, with things
that are good for you and your higher self.

Set your intentions for your day every day.

Wake up with a smile and a positive intention to make your day great.

It's your choice what kind of day you have today, not anyone else's.

You have to choose your happiness every day.

You have to see that you are worthy of love
and happiness on your path.

Your day is yours and no one else's.

Your choices are yours and no one else's.

You are being blessed in every moment and in every step.

See the blessings, the love, and the beauty of your life on your path.

Feel and embrace today.

Your day is your day, not anyone else's.

Day 251

You are consciousness.

You are awareness.

You just are.

You have no name, no labels, no age, no beliefs, no religion, and no gender; this is who you truly are.

You are awareness, the energy of the universe, and God.

When you sit in meditation and just be, with nothing in your mind, you are experiencing your true self.

Just be.

Stop trying to be someone when truly you are no one.

You just are.

This body is just a vessel to create a life in.

There is nothing more to life than to just be, with no identity.

You are just energy.

You are no one.

If you can let go of your identity of who you think you are, you will have a new perspective on life.

You just have to be.

You are no one.

You are nothing.

You just are.

Day 252

Life isn't about what you have, it's about how you feel inside.

Life is a feeling.

Life is the feeling of love inside.

Love is your life.

To have a great life, you have to have your heart on your path.

Your heart must be open to give and receive love on your path.

Love is the basis of everything in you and around you.

Life isn't about acquiring material things.

Life is about loving what you already have in your life.

That's what will make you feel whole.

Loving who you are and what's inside of you, that's what life really is.

Life isn't outside of you.

Life is in your heart and soul.

Life is love.

Love is life.

When you see what's on the inside of you, you can love
life anywhere you go and with anything you have.

You don't need anything to have love in your
life, except for love for yourself.

Day 253

Don't give your past power anymore.

Learn what you need to from it and keep going.

The past is gone.

It can't hurt you anymore unless you keep looking at it.

If you focus on the hurt, you bring that into the present moment.

That hurt is just an illusion now because it is not here.

It's done.

Know that it is gone.

Learn what you have to in every moment.

Then let the rest go.

Learning from your past is the gift of life.

That's what we are all here to do.

To learn, grow, evolve, and create.

To be happy, at peace, and in love with yourself,
your path, and the choices that you make.

Stop letting someone or something control
your life that is not here anymore.

Holding on to grudges, resentments, hate, and anger
is what is ruining your own life, no one else's.

It's all an illusion that you need to let go of.

Stop hurting yourself and live in unconditional love, peace,
and happiness because that is where your true life is.

That's your true self.

Peace, love, bliss, joy, and happiness.

Start feeling all of those feelings instead.

They will change your life.

Then you will grow, evolve, and change, when you see the truth.

Day 254

Start your day by giving thanks and appreciation to yourself.

Start your day by telling yourself how proud
you are of all that you are doing.

You are doing it.

You are rocking it.

You are on fire.

Start your day by giving thanks to all the support
and guidance you have in your life.

Start your day by asking for help, guidance, and support
from the universe, God, spirit guides, angels, and ascended
masters that are with you every day by your side.

They will help you when you ask them sincerely.

Acknowledge them in your day, and look for signs and messages that
they show you to let you know they are here for you and with you.

Start your day off with thanks and appreciation
for your life and your path.

Appreciation and thankfulness for all that you have
and all that you are helps to change your life.

Have an amazing day.

Day 255

Triggers tell you a lot.

They show you the truth of where you need
to heal and work on yourself.

If someone or something or a situation is triggering you into
negative emotions, ask yourself why this is happening.

This is always showing you where you need to let
go, change your perspective, step back, look inside
yourself, change your mindset, and be aware.

There is always something for you to learn
and grow from in every situation.

Triggers are things that are not truly healed inside
of you, even though you thought they were.

There are always more layers that have to be
peeled away and exposed in the light.

Keep reflecting; keep asking; keep healing.

Work out the toxic parts of you and let them go.

Then you can be free, and you can move forward into a new you.

Day 256

Stop looking for love in others, and start looking for it in yourself.

Stop trying, and start doing.

Life is amazing once you see it from the eyes of love.

Where do you think God is?

Who do you think God is?

Do you believe there is a God?

There is.

You are God.

God is inside of you.

Always.

God is energy, and we are made of that energy.

It's in every one of us.

You cannot feel the energy of God's love flowing to you when
you stop loving yourself, even though it's still in you.

God's energy is on the love side of you, not the hate or depressed side.

When you start loving yourself again, you will feel
God's energy strongly because you will be closer to
the love that He is giving you all the time.

You will be aligned with the energy of God and your true self.

You will feel love, and you will never feel alone again.

This is the most important thing you can begin to do today.

Start speaking to yourself positively; God would never put you
down or say or think angry thoughts about you or others.

Because you are one together, and God is
always on the love side of you.

God never wavers from unconditional love.

Love yourself, and align with God, who is inside of
you, and change your path and life today.

You have the power inside of you.

Loving yourself is your true power that God wants
you to feel and know and align with today.

Day 257

It's our turn now to change.

It's our turn now to choose happiness.

It's our turn now to be wise.

It's our turn now to be compassionate.

It's our turn now to love unconditionally.

It's our turn now to create peace.

It's our turn now to awaken.

It's our turn now to change the world as we know it.

The time is now, and it's our turn to awaken to the truth.

Let's start now.

It's time.

Day 258

Boundaries are for you.

If you don't have any, others will walk all over you.

You need to keep your boundaries and not let others cross them.

They are there for your own well-being, not theirs.

Boundaries stop you from toxic behaviour.

They keep you from allowing toxic people
to abuse and manipulate you.

It's important to have healthy boundaries and
not to let people step over the line.

Tell them they are when they do.

They may not like it, but it's about you, not them.

If they don't like it, then they have the problem of not respecting other
people's boundaries, and they probably do it to everyone else as well.

They need to learn that lesson, and you are
setting boundaries to show them that.

Boundaries are about respect.

Respect yourself enough to have boundaries in your
life, and make sure you stick with them.

Day 259

Today and everyday love who you are.

Love yourself.

Be authentic and true to you.

You get what you are.

Work on yourself.

Let the universe bring in your life.

Trust and faith.

You will manifest things in your life that you want
when you have no doubts and no resistance.

Love your life, yourself, and your path.

This is what you need to do in order for everything
you want in your life to manifest.

Unconditional love, trusting, being positive, and letting go of
doubt make a big difference in what comes to you on your path.

Day 260

Change yourself because that's all you can do.

You cannot change other people, especially those
who cannot see that they are toxic to others.

You have to look after you.

Choose yourself.

Love yourself enough not to be hurt by others, by situations and
relationships that are not going anywhere and are not serving you.

Let them go, love them from afar, and wish them the best.

You can still love them, but you can't stay directly in their life.

You cannot change another.

You have to accept things for what they are
and people for who they are.

Start to change, and you will see the light in others
that resonates with you on your path.

Day 261

Let your thoughts flow with love.

Go easy on yourself today.

Rest if you feel like it.

Slow down.

Take some time for you in the day.

Rest.

Recharge.

Relax.

You don't have to do it all.

You don't have to be a superhero and save everyone today.

Save yourself.

Don't forget about you.

Do you put yourself last and everyone else first?

Do it the other way around.

You first, then others.

Rest.

Recharge.

Relax.

Let someone help you today.

You don't always need to be the saviour, the peacekeeper, the hero.

Let someone else do the work today.

Life gets busy, and you race around.

But you need to stop and put your feet up sometimes.

Everything will get done.

Pace yourself.

Feel what you want to do today.

What is your heart telling you to do?

Follow your heart, and let it lead your path.

It will look after you better than your racing mind.

Enjoy your day.

Stay in the present moment, doing all that you love to do.

Have fun.

Life is fun.

Life is beautiful.

Day 262

We need to learn to accept people for who they are.

We have all been there before.

We are not perfect.

If we are judging someone, then that's where we need to heal.

That's what judgement is.

A reflection of what's in us, we are seeing in them.

So, learn to love everyone unconditionally.

Even yourself

Especially yourself.

Day 263

You need to be aware of patterns you keep repeating.

They keep you stuck in your life, going around
and around on a merry-go-round.

The only way off is to look at yourself, your behaviour, what you
are allowing in your life, and what you are giving to others.

If you are not showing up for yourself in your life,
then you are not healing, growing, or evolving.

To grow you need to see the toxic patterns you
are allowing in your life and stop them.

You need to have boundaries and stick to them
and not allow others to take advantage.

If you don't do this, the situations will repeat, just
with different people and circumstances.

Self-awareness is key to stopping the merry-go-round.

Get off, learn and then go forward.

Evolve, don't repeat.

Day 264

Once you have awakened to the truth and to who you really are, don't let anyone drag you back into the chaos and ego.

You worked too hard on your self-worth and

self-respect.

Keep the boundaries you have set.

They are for you and your mental well-being.

Keep moving forward, and don't look back.

You are not going that way anymore.

Life is in front of you, unfolding every day.

People will have to catch up with you.

They will need to do their own self-work
and find their own truth and love.

Day 265

There is no ending to life.

You are working, learning, and processing it.

There is always more.

You are living it, and you are doing it.

Don't ever think that you are not.

You are slowly moving forward into the new.

That is what we are all doing.

There is always going to be something more
to learn, to know, and to experience.

All of our paths lead back to the same spot.

Home.

We are all on a journey back home to God.

There is no wrong path.

They all lead back to home.

Some paths we choose are more difficult than others.

We are all on the same journey, just with
different views and perspectives.

We are never on the wrong path.

God is always steering us home.

Let's live every day being happy, knowing
that we are going the right way.

God is waiting for us, no matter how long
the journey is or where it takes us.

Day 266

Be the best you can be on this beautiful day.

Be grateful and appreciative for all that you receive
in your day and for all that you already have.

Choose to be happy today.

Choose to be kind today.

Choose to love everyone and everything, even if it hurts.

See the love in it.

Choose to be who you are today.

Be authentic.

Love yourself.

Love others.

Most importantly, be happy and see the beauty
in you and in everything you do.

Enjoy today.

Day 267

Self-awareness of your thoughts is the key to
healing and changing your mindset.

Awareness of how you speak to yourself, and others is important.

Have awareness of negative thoughts.

Have awareness of your emotions.

Why? Who? What? Where? When? How?

Why is this thought here?

Who is this thought about? Me? Or someone else?

What triggered this emotion or thought?

Where is this thought going?

Is it going down a negative or positive path?

Where did it come from? My ego? Or my soul?

When did this happen? Past? Future? Present?

How can I learn from this thought or emotion?

How can I let this go?

How is this hurting me and making me suffer?

These are some examples of self-awareness questions to think about, to
help you process and acknowledge your thoughts, actions, and mindset.

If you become aware of what's in your mind, you can change your life.

You can let go of the unnecessary egoic
thoughts if you are aware of them.

Self-awareness is the key to healing, letting go, and changing your life.

Day 268

We all walk our own path in our own unique way.

We make different choices than others, love different things, have different passions, different goals, and different perspectives.

We are all so different, walking our own path to happiness and love.

We all have the same destination, but we get there from different directions.

Stop comparing your path to others.

You are not like anyone else.

Your journey is your own.

Love it.

Day 269

Your love and your light are so bright.

You should see and know that.

It will help you illuminate the darkness on your
path that is overwhelming you with fear.

Today fear doesn't stand a chance because of
your light that shines so bright.

Turn on the light with your smile, your heart, your
excitement, your joy, your happiness, your love for
yourself, and for the love of God's light in you.

Shine that light bright today, to wash over the darkness.

Darkness on your path is an illusion because you are light.

You are love, and you are light.

Darkness cannot see in your light because it is so beautiful and bright.

You now have put the darkness in fear of your light.

It's repelled.

Your light is in you to activate and to keep shining.

You don't ever have to turn it off.

It's meant to stay on and light up your path and
life and to help light up others' path.

Love this light in you because it sparks more light all around you.

Your light turns on other lights.

It attracts more light to you.

Be bright today; it's needed so much.

The world needs your light to shine today.

Shine bright in the dark for all those around

you so that they can see your light and step

out of their fear.

It's in you to give and to share.

Shine and be bright.

Smile today; be happy, laugh, and give, and God's
light will replenish your light always.

Day 270

Do something for you today.

Self-care is the most important part of every day.

It's for you.

It replenishes and recharges you.

Self-care helps you to fill your heart up again with your love.

The love you have for yourself and your path.

Self-care and self-love are for you.

You cannot keep giving and giving and giving.

You will drain your energy, and you will be depleted.

You need to refill every day to give to others.

You need to rest, recharge, and reboot.

You can't keep functioning on empty.

Your car won't run without gas.

You need to refill it.

You need to do the same with yourself.

You do it with your own love and energy.

If you don't love yourself unconditionally,
there is no love in you to fill up with.

No love for yourself means you can't refill your own heart.

Your love for you is the most important
thing you can receive in your day.

It's a gift for yourself.

It's a gift from God.

How can you receive this give of loving yourself?

Forgive yourself.

You block that love if you hate yourself for your past
mistakes, for hurting others, for negative self-talk,
and for doing things you don't want to do.

Forgiving yourself is important to help love start flowing to you again.

Stop blocking your love and God's love.

Start doing something you love every day.

Your passions and hobbies are things that take you to a
place of enjoyment, happiness, excitement, and love.

Do something for you in your day.

Going for a walk and being out in nature
pours the love of God into you.

It's connected to you.

You are a part of earth's beautiful nature, and you need to enjoy it.

Connect to it every day.

Meditation is so important as well.

Sit in meditation every day to experience who you truly are.

You just are.

You are nothing but a soul full of God's love, and that love is pouring
into you and filling you up when you are aligned with his love.

You will feel love in meditation, and it will fill you up.

Every day you have to choose to fill yourself up in
a way that aligns and resonates with you.

These tasks should be a routine part of your day.

Take time to refill every day, otherwise you will be
running on empty and not serving yourself.

You will drain your energy and become toxic and sick if you
don't start doing something for yourself every single day.

Loving yourself is the most important thing can do for you every day.

It changes your life and your path.

Love changes you.

Day 271

Affirm this:

I love myself fully today for who I am.

I forgive myself fully today for my past mistakes.

I let them go.

They helped me to learn and to grow and to see a new way.

I forgive my past.

It cannot hurt me anymore.

I forgive the people that hurt me.

They can no longer give me pain.

I forgive them for they are like me, learning and growing.

Every situation and person in my life shows me a new way to be.

They show me a new way to love myself unconditionally.

I am who I am becoming because of my past.

It cannot hurt me today but only make me better and better.

My past is gone.

I only have the now.

I only have me to see and change into someone
better than I was yesterday.

My past is gone.

I love how it is changing me into the beautiful
person that I am becoming.

I am growing and learning from everyone and everything around me.

I truly appreciate these experiences from my past.

They have changed my life.

I love my life and who I have become today.

Thank you past for teaching me today.

You have taught me to love myself and to
accept myself for who I am now.

Day 272

When you pray for something, you must be in alignment
with God's love to hear the messages he is giving you.

You will not hear the messages God sends you if
you are out of alignment with his love.

God's unconditional love, vibration, and energy are always unwavering.

When you feel sad and hurt, you are out of alignment with God's love.

God will never go down in vibration into a
state of worry or fear with you.

You have to change and choose the vibration of love.

Love for you, your life, and your path.

The only way to do this is to let go of your past, love others
and yourself, and forgive others and yourself on your path.

Forgiveness is the key to happiness and to being in a state of love.

Love is alignment with God's energy, not worry, fear, or hate.

You cannot hear God from that state.

You are out of alignment.

God is in you, showing you the way through an open heart of love.

Fear and worry close your heart to feeling God.

When you feel God and are aligned with His love,
you will never feel alone on your path again.

You won't feel sad, unhappy, unloved, angry, or in fear.

If you become out of alignment, those are the
feelings that will be present in you.

When you are in alignment, you will feel
deep love, joy, happiness, and bliss.

You will hear God's messages.

You will hear and see the answers to your prayers.

Start forgiving, and start loving who you are and your path.

Start loving the now.

Start living in the now because that is where
God's love is for you always.

Day 273

Don't compare yourself to others, that's not a good thing on your path.

You are a unique individual.

You are not the same as anyone else in any way, shape, or form.

You are you, and they are them.

Don't follow the crowd.

Be you.

Step into your own path, your own way, with your own style.

Stop thinking you are mediocre; you are not.

What you focus on is what you get on your path.

Your path is your path.

Follow your own.

Stop comparing yourself to others; no one is like you.

No one.

You are amazing, and you are brave for walking your own unique path.

Step into it.

Own it.

Be you.

You got this.

Be you, not someone you're not.

Day 274

Everything in your life starts with you.

Not anywhere else.

All the answers are within you.

If you want clarity, ask for it.

If you want love, ask for it.

If you want trust, ask for it.

If you want peace, ask for it.

If you want happiness, ask for it.

You are never alone.

Asking God for guidance, support, and help to lead you on
your path is the first thing you should do each morning.

And then let it in.

Trust and faith are needed, not worry, doubt, and fear.

Worry, doubt, and fear only block the help you are asking for.

Alignment with God's energy is important when
wanting to bring more into your life.

Alignment with love for yourself, your path,
and your life lets you move forward.

It's a state of allowing, a state of flow, and a state of surrendering.

Alignment and allowing things to flow to you instead of
resisting them with worry and fear will get you everywhere.

Fear is not helping you on your path.

Fear is blocking you on your path.

Love is always flowing to you from the energy
of God, for you to use within yourself.

Let go of fear.

Grab hold of the love inside of you that is flowing
to you from God every moment of your life.

Love is the way to everything.

Love is you.

Love will heal your heart and move you forward
into a new path and a better person.

Day 275

You have to live in the moment day by day, and life will unfold.

All the things that you are led to are leading you to
your passions and your purpose on your path.

That is why you have to patient and let life flow to you.

Choose the path that says yes to you, and
let go of the path that says no.

Don't look at the old path anymore.

It is not meant for you.

What you are meant for will come to you.

When you live in the moment and stop resisting it
with unhappiness, hate, disappointment, and all other
negative emotions, you can let this new path in.

It will find you.

You will find it.

God will lead you.

You need to follow your heart because that is
where your life, purpose, and passions are.

Let your heart lead your life.

It will always lead you to the higher path.

Beauty Glows Everywhere

This piece is one of my favourites as well.

It draws me into the glow of the sun that brings life to all of us.

Beauty is everywhere; we just have to stop and look around us.

It is there for us to enjoy, to absorb, and to love.

Stop and see the glow of life. This butterfly is basking
in the sun that is giving it a life to live.

Day 276

Oneness is coming; we will be one.

We will work together.

We will love one another equally.

We will support each other.

We will live in peace and harmony and love.

We will know that we are all equal but that
we are also individual and unique.

We are joined as one, as we are all made of love.

We are not separate.

The love of God that creates our soul is in all of us.

We are all God's children, and we are made of that love.

The world will align with this love.

The world is shifting into this love now.

We are shifting.

Can you feel it?

It all starts with you, shifting into love.

Love for yourself, for the earth, for the universe,
for God, for your path, and for your life.

Love is oneness.

Love is alignment.

Love is melding everyone together.

Love is the core of us, the earth, and the universe.

Do you feel it?

Love is here.

Start loving you.

Start feeling the truth of who you are.

Love is the truth.

Everything else is an illusion.

When you shift your mindset to look at all
the love, your whole world changes.

Love is here; it always was.

It never left.

The world just looked away from love.

Walked away from it.

And didn't choose it.

Now is the time to choose love.

The world is shifting into love right now, and so are you.

Be aligned with love.

Stay aligned.

Love is here.

It is always here for you.

Day 277

Change means something new is coming.

Change means better things are coming.

Change means a shift in perspective.

Change is always showing you something that
you need to alter about yourself.

That you need to let go of something.

That you need to see something in a different way.

Change is good if you can see what it is doing
for you on your path and in your life.

It shifts you into a beautiful new person.

Change is coming for all of us.

You are shifting into something new every day.

You have to move forward, become better, become new.

If you don't change, you are stuck, and you are
not being true to who you really are.

A new life will flow to you when you stop holding
on to the past and who you once were.

You are not the same person as yesterday, and
you will be different again tomorrow.

You can change every day if you let the new life that
you are moving forward to into your path.

The saying is "out with the old and in with the new" for a reason.

It's very true.

Embrace the new day and the new path every day.

You don't know what is next for you.

But you cannot remain the same.

Change your perspective, way, direction, and who you are if
you are feeling that something better is coming for you.

Don't hold on to the past, to the old energy of who
you once were, or you will never move forward.

Change is good and is going to happen, so let it flow to you and
let it take you to new places, new scenery, and new outlooks.

Change happens to everyone, and that's how you
will grow and become better every day.

Day 278

We are here for higher knowing, healing, and letting go of the past.

We are here to let go of worry.

We are here to learn to trust and have faith in the universe and God.

We are here to love and live in a new way.

We are here to become new and to be different.

We are here to learn, grow, evolve, and
expand our minds and awareness.

We are here to live in awareness instead of unconsciously.

We are here to see the truth of our existence.

The world needs new perspectives, higher levels
of consciousness, and for us to awaken.

We are all here together, changing the world we live in.

Day 279

Be proud of yourself.

Believe in yourself.

That's where you start.

If you're not proud of yourself, how is anyone
else going to be proud of you?

Be proud of yourself, and others will see that in you.

Don't put your happiness in someone else's hands.

You're giving your power away, when you want
others to see you for who you are.

Do it for yourself.

You need to know it, believe it, be it, show it,
and see that you are worthy of it.

Be proud of you, who you are, where you are
going, and what you are doing.

Be proud to be you.

Don't let anyone take that away from you.

They don't know you.

You are strong, confident, standing tall, and
taking care of yourself and your path.

Live for you, and not for other people.

Live for you, and be proud of yourself.

You're the only one who counts.

Look around at everything happening in the world.

It's truly beautiful and amazing the way the world works.

The sun and the moon rise and fall.

The trees and flowers grow and die when they need to.

The birds, insects, and animals know what they need to do to keep going, and they have everything provided for them.

It's a miracle to see and watch this happening every day.

It's a miracle.

Most of us are not even noticing or paying attention to this.

It's a miracle that everything has a place and part in this universe.

We are miracles.

Our bodies run like machines, and we take that for granted.

We are creating more humans every day, and
that is truly an amazing miracle.

We hear, smell, taste, see, feel, and know.

Those are amazing parts of us that we take for granted.

Our blood flows; our organs function; we breath; we think;
we digest food, without even having to do anything.

It's so amazing that we have these beautiful bodies on this
earth, and we literally don't even appreciate them.

We need to start taking notice of these things that
function without us even having to do anything.

How life works, creates, and just is, is truly amazing.

Every day is a miracle, and miracles are all around us, and even in us.

It's truly beautiful, the miracles that are in front of us
every day, some even looking at us in the mirror.

Because we are miracles.

So, appreciate all the miracles going on around
you, and look at life through God's eyes.

Day 281

Be unique and you.

Be genuine and authentic.

Start doing your own thing.

The people that resonate with that will love you for being you.

Being you is easier than being fake for others.

Pleasing your own self is more rewarding.

Take yourself back.

Be you always.

Day 282

It's time to start changing your perspectives,
your words, and your mindsets.

If you are having a hard time, it's because you
are choosing to think it is hard.

Focussing on a problem only brings more problems.

Focussing on hardship, chaos, anger, regrets, depression, anxiety,
and fear only brings more and more of that to your path and life.

You attract what you focus on.

When you focus on love, peace, happiness, trust, faith, joy, and
ease and flow, you bring more of that into your path and life.

When you say words like: "This is too hard," "I am trying,"
"I am struggling," or "Why can't I do this?" these are all
negative statements that you are affirming into your life.

Change your words to: "I know I will be able to do this,"
"I am capable of doing this," and "I can do this."

These are a few other affirmations:

"I love that I can do and be whatever I put my mind and focus on."

"I am taking my life one step at a time."

"I don't have to be overwhelmed by the whole
picture; I just have to live in the moment."

So, choose your words and perspectives wisely.

What you say and do directly affects every aspect of your life every day.

Stay focussed on the positive.

Have faith and trust in the universe to get
you to where you want to be.

Day 283

Affirm this:

I am excited for this day and every day.

I am excited to experience what I am going
to experience today and every day.

Thank you for bringing me this new day to experience.

Thank you for everything I will receive today.

I am truly blessed to be here to experience
and explore a new day, all day.

Thank you for this new day.

Day 284

We are all divinely guided.

We are all divinity.

We are all eternal.

We are all souls.

We are not of the planet; we are a part of the amazing universe.

We are here to experience and create for God so
God can experience our creations with us.

We are here to learn soul lessons.

We are here to learn our karmic soul lessons.

We are here for love, peace, joy, bliss, and unconditional
love because that's what our true essence is, our soul.

That's who we truly are.

We are souls having a human experience, that's why we are truly here.

Day 285

You have to believe in yourself.

You can't just say it.

You have to change as well.

You have to heal yourself.

Start loving yourself, forgiving yourself.

When you are in a negative vibration, your
outside world becomes negative as well.

You have to do the work involved in changing your mindset.

You have to believe it.

If you truly don't believe that you can change your mindset,
then your outside world will reflect that to you.

What you focus on, you get in your life.

If you don't believe in yourself, your vibration
will draw that into your path.

You have to work on that every day for the rest of your life.

You have to choose our own happiness, energy, and vibration every day.

Choose to be positive, and choose to change on the inside as well.

You can't pretend the universe knows your
true emotions, energy, and vibration.

It knows vibrations only.

Start taking charge of your life.

Start showing up for yourself every day.

Start believing in yourself, your path, and your life.

Day 286

When you can't let go of something, it is only hurting you.

When you're not letting go of something that means
you are not letting in anything either.

You are missing out on an amazing life because you have a strong
hold on the past or something that is no longer serving you.

What do you think you are missing out on?

You are missing out on happiness, freedom, bliss, joy, beauty,
ease and flow, calmness, peace, and much more like this.

Is it worth it to miss out on all these great
things that will change your life?

Look forward, not backward.

Live in the now.

Live in the present moment.

Let your best life flow into you.

It's here for you, but you have to choose it.

You are missing out on life.

Live for today, and let go of what is gone.

You are only hurting yourself and suffering in the now because of it.

This life now is so beautiful.

Enjoy it.

Feel it.

See it.

Live it.

Day 287

If you don't like a person for what they are doing
or how they are living, that's on you.

You are in judgement, hate, and in your ego.

You are what they are.

You have attracted them with your energy and vibration.

You are the same vibration and energy.

They are a reflection of what is in you.

The only way to heal this is by looking at the
opposite emotion of judgement.

Forgiveness.

Forgive yourself and forgive them.

This will allow love to flow into you and the other person.

You will help both of you with forgiveness.

You flow your energy of love to them and to yourself.

You will unblock your path and start the healing process on your path.

You won't be in judgement anymore, and you
will have raised your vibration to love.

You don't have to condone the others' actions, but
you will be able to accept it and let it go.

It won't trigger you anymore.

You can let that person or problem go.

This is how you can love everyone unconditionally on your path.

Turning judgement and hate into forgiveness, acceptance, and unconditional love changes you.

This is how you can heal your heart and your past so that you can raise your vibration, change your energy, and change your life into a better path and you.

$\mathcal{Day}$ 288

Being alone changes you if you see that you need to find yourself again.

Being alone is beautiful when you start to change yourself.

Embrace it.

You will find and love your passions and your purpose again.

Healing shows you the way to those.

Loving yourself shows you a new way of living and loving your path, yourself, and others.

Being alone only feels bad because you are lost.

You need to heal and find your way again.

Do the things you love to do.

Connect with God and nature, and you will start to see the truth, your purpose, and your love for you again.

$\mathcal{D}ay$ 289

When you are living for other people, you are draining yourself.

When you don't know how to say no, that you are not available to do something or that you are emotionally unavailable to help someone, you drain your own energy for others.

You pay the price for becoming a people pleaser.

Saying no sometimes is healthy.

Saying yes all the time, especially when you want to say no, is toxic behaviour.

Choose yourself first, then if you have rested, recharged, rebooted, and reenergized your mind, body, and soul, say yes to others.

If you have given and given over and over again to others and not to yourself, then you will need to stop.

You don't need to be a hero, superstar, or martyr; this is unhealthy behaviour.

Take charge of you, your life, your path, your energy, and your vibration.

It's super important to look after you first, then others.

You first, then others.

It makes a difference in your life.

There will be less stress, fatigue, and worry.

There will be more energy, clarity, and focus when you are recharged, rebooted, and rested.

Alignment with yourself and loving who you are is the best place you can be to help others and to create less stress in your life.

Remember: you first, then others.

Day 290

Look at you, standing there all tall and proud.

You are changing.

Your mindset is different; it's better.

You are feeling different.

You have a different energy and vibration;
they are lighter and more positive.

You are learning new things.

You are discovering who you truly are every day.

You are changing your habits, letting go of old ways.

You are stepping up and into a new person.

Look at you; you are growing, learning, changing,
and evolving into a new mindset.

You are feeling happy and energized.

You are proud, confident, growing, and radiating love all over.

Look at you; you are doing it.

You are changing.

$\mathcal{D}ay$ 291

You have a destiny that you have come to fulfill in your life.

That's why you came here.

To create a life that you can follow though to this destiny.

Your life has been predetermined before you came
here with other souls to help fulfill this destiny.

If you try to stop it, or if you are on a different path,
the universe will put roadblocks in your way.

You can choose not to fulfill your destiny with free will, but you will
miss out on this beautiful path and your journey will be difficult.

You will have to do it again in another lifetime.

Trying to suppress it or change it will only
create challenges on your path.

That's why listening to your intuition is important
because it is guiding you to that destiny plus other
beautiful things that you are here to learn.

Lead with your heart and your intuition.

Listen to it.

Follow it.

Feel it in your heart; that this is the way you want and need to go.

Don't let others stop you.

They have their own destiny and path to follow.

Your destiny is your own in every lifetime you live on this earth.

Follow your destiny.

Day 292

Happiness, true happiness, starts with you and your love
for yourself, your path, and the life that you live.

Happiness is deep love for yourself and knowing who you are.

Happiness always comes from within yourself.

No one else can give you this deep love, happiness,
joy, and peace but you and God.

The only other place it comes from is God.

Pure happiness comes from your alignment
with God's energy and your energy.

This is the way to pure, deep happiness and love within you.

Because you are one with God.

God is flowing and pouring that unconditional
love through you always.

Feel it; receive it; be blessed by this love that
will fill your heart and never leave you.

Happiness is only within you because of the love from you and God.

That's pure alignment flowing.

It makes it grow and spread all around you, everywhere you go.

It makes you fill up with happiness and love.

It's in each and every one of us in that way.

When you see yourself through God's love and perspective, you
will see the world and yourself from that perspective as well.

Deep love for yourself and for God changes the world around you
and how you perceive your life, your path, and who you truly are.

Happiness comes from deep within.

That's where is starts.

In you and with the love of God.

Day 293

Your power is now.

This can't be stressed this enough.

The power is now.

Live in the moment.

Live day by day.

Let life come to you.

Make choices as they come.

You only have three choices.

Accept it.

Change it.

Leave it.

Life is simple.

You are making it too complicated.

You are here to create your life, not to suffer or live in fear.

You are here to love life and live in the
moment and create life as it comes.

Day 294

Your life starts with you.

Work on yourself every day.

Do the inner work to heal.

Stop looking at everyone else and what they are doing.

You change your path by doing your own work.

It starts with you.

Nowhere else.

You progress this way, and by living your true authentic
path, you also help others in the process.

Stop looking at everyone else's path, and just look at your own.

That's how to progress forward.

That's how to start changing your life.

And that's how the world will start to change.

With one person at a time. changing their life to an authentic one.

It starts with you.

Day 295

Believe in yourself.

Believe in who you are becoming.

Believe that you can do it.

Believe that nothing will stop you.

No one can stop you, only you.

Show up for yourself, and do the things you say you are going to do.

You are the only one in charge.

Only you are in charge of your life, your path, and where you are going.

Choose you.

Be the person you want to be.

Believe it.

Know it.

Live it.

Become it.

Believe in yourself.

Day 296

The beginning is always now.

The new is there in every moment.

Every day is a new chance to step into your truth
and to discover who you truly are.

You are here to create things you love and
enjoy every moment of your life.

You are here every day to help other people on their
path as well, co-creating things together.

You are here every day to move forward into the new.

Every moment is new and in the now.

The only chance you have to live your fullest life
is in the now, today, and in this moment.

Today is always a new beginning.

Love it; live in it; choose it.

Be here in the now and enjoy every moment.

The beginning is always now.

Day 297

To help yourself heal you have to go within
and find what is causing the pain.

Your pain needs to be healed.

It needs to be looked at with love, compassion,
kindness, and forgiveness.

Don't look at it with hate, anger, resentment, or disappointment.

This only fuels the fire.

It turns it into more pain.

You project that pain outwardly to others on your path, hurting them.

And yourself.

Your pain needs to be healed in order to move forward.

You need to let it go.

You have to see the source of it and the pattern
that keeps it going and living inside of you.

Pain can cause so much destruction on your path if you let it grow.

Depression, addiction to alcohol, drugs, food, sex,
and smoking, toxic relationships, and more are just
some of the ways it manifests on your path.

These are all negative outlets used as a crutch to ease the
pain, but they are only adding to it, not lessening it.

You are bypassing it by trying to cope with
more toxic behaviour and patterns.

Instead of loving yourself and whoever or whatever
caused this pain or asking for help from God, you pour
your sorrows into toxic substances or behaviours.

Self-love and forgiveness are the keys to healing these negative behaviours and letting go of your addictions and toxicity.

Looking inwardly at yourself with unconditional love, compassion, and kindness instead of outwardly at the world with hate and blaming others for your pain can heal your heart.

Your pain is your pain, not anyone else's.

You're hurting because of the decisions you made on your path, but you have the choice to respond or react in every situation.

Unhealthy, unhealed people almost always react to a situation or a person.

You are triggered.

Those triggers need to be healed.

Healed with love, not with addictions, negativity, or more toxicity.

They are showing you where you need to heal on your path.

See them as a lesson to learn, to grow, and to change from.

That's what they are showing you.

These triggers help you if you are aware of them.

Most people are not, and they just blindly project that trigger, blame someone else, and cope with the pain by pouring themselves into more unhealthy behaviours and addictions.

Loving yourself deeply and forgiving yourself and others are solutions to these behaviours, addictions, and toxic patterns.

Loving God is also a very important step in healing.

God is pouring love out to you, but you are blocking it and not feeling it, as you are not in alignment with His love because of your toxic behaviours.

When you start to love yourself deeply, you will not want to hurt yourself or another else anymore.

You will be in alignment as well now with
the unconditional love of God.

That love will help you heal tremendously on your path.

God is always there, unwavering, yet you turn away from
it when you don't love yourself as God does with that
energy you are receiving, always of unconditional love.

You will have self-respect, self-love, self-worth, compassion,
kindness, and unconditional love for yourself now.

You will become addicted to the feeling of
unconditional love for yourself and your path.

This healing yourself.

This is alignment of your true self.

Pouring love into your heart that you are missing
because you haven't been giving it to yourself first.

You haven't been choosing yourself first.

You have been choosing toxicity and addiction over love.

That's false love.

Love changes you.

Love heals you.

Love makes you whole.

God's love, your love, helps you to heal your wounds
and lets you move forward into a new, amazing life that
is waiting for you on the other side of that pain.

Love yourself.

Change your whole life.

Day 298

Everyone has a part in every path you are on.

In a toxic, abusive relationship, you both play a part in it.

You, the victim, are learning a lesson on your path, while
the abuser is also learning a lesson on theirs.

It's accountability for your actions and their actions as well.

There is no blame in either part.

And yes, there is hurt and pain.

Everyone is learning lessons to evolve and grow.

People come together to show what they need to heal in each other.

Abuse is not being condoned here or justified in any way.

This is just helping you to see the why behind it, and
the reason why these relationships come together.

Abuse is never acceptable.

It's never the answer.

No one deserves any kind of abuse.

The faster you understand this, the faster you can seek
healing and love and learn for the next path.

This is why it is so important to heal from a relationship first,
so you don't repeat the same lessons in the next person.

If you didn't heal and learn from this, you will be doing
it all over again and being hurt all over again.

Abuse is not acceptable behaviour, but it's sometimes
reality and there are reasons why it happens.

Both people are not healed.

Both people are toxic in some way.

Both people have a part in this.

Both people have to go within and heal.

You cannot heal in the same environment that hurt you.

When the lesson is learned, the healing process can begin.

Deep love and forgiveness can take place.

There is no blame in anything in life, only
lessons and growing and evolving.

That is why situations and people are here and showing up for you.

To heal, and to grow.

Both people need it.

That's why it's so important to heal before
moving on to the next person.

So you don't repeat patterns, so you can heal, learn,
grow, and become a better person on your path, and so
you can have a healthy relationship with another.

Day 299

Peace is the ultimate place to be in.

Peace is beautiful.

Peace is the centre of life.

Peace is alignment with yourself and God.

Peace is freedom.

Peace is heaven.

Day 300

Everything you are looking for is inside of you.

You are made with it inside of you.

The solution to everything you need is inside your soul.

It knows the answers and is guiding you,
moving you through life toward them.

It is also guiding you to your purpose, lessons, soul mates, and destiny.

Your soul knows everything.

You need to take a break from your busy life and
mind and let these solutions and answers in.

Meditation, connecting with nature, doing things you love,
they are all bringing you into alignment with your soul.

In this place of alignment, you receive what you need to know.

Slow down to let those answers come.

Open your mind on your path to hear the guidance.

When you are busy, you can't hear your soul clearly.

When you are quiet, you can hear the inner guidance clearly.

We are all being divinely guided every day to
everything we want, need, desire, and love.

Just stop and listen every day, and you will hear everything.

Day 301

You have to unfold your wings if you want to soar on to new paths.

You have to break free of the heavy thoughts, feelings, people, behaviours, addictions, and negative mindsets that worry you.

All negative energy is heavy.

All positive energy is light.

So, if you want to fly seriously, you have to let go of that heavy energy.

Then you will soar higher and higher.

$\mathcal{D}ay$ 302

If you want to change, you have to choose to be different.

That means giving up toxic things, behaviours, people, and addictions.

That means facing your own demons as well.

Choosing yourself first over others.

Change means choosing yourself and who you want to become instead of choosing old toxic behaviours or people that show up on your path.

It's a choice.

It's not an easy choice; it will be challenging but well worth it.

It will be rewarding once you see yourself differently and feel differently about yourself.

Choose the better choices.

Choose the better you.

Change is worth it.

Day 303

You can always ask for help.

Help is always here for you.

When you ask the universe for help, it always answers you.

But you have to ask.

You have to ask from a place of love and a place of trust
and faith that God has you in His hands and is guiding you,
leading you, and pointing you in the right direction.

You have to be in a place of appreciation, love, and
gratitude in order to hear His guidance and help.

This is the vibration of the universe, of God, and
this is the vibration they are always at.

In order to hear and see the messages, which come in a magnitude
of ways, you need to be in alignment with that vibration.

If you stay in the vibration of love, appreciation,
gratitude, joy, bliss, happiness, trust, and faith, then
you will be at the same vibration as God.

At this level, you are in alignment.

At this level, you can feel the love of the universe
all around you, in you, and through you.

At this level, you can receive the answers to your prayers.

There is always help out there for you.

You are never alone.

You are divinely guided by God and your spirit guides.

That's where heaven is, in alignment with God's energy.

That is pure alignment and where heaven on earth is.

Day 304

If you are feeling confused, thinking you're going the wrong direction, doubting yourself, or don't know the way, trust your gut instinct.

That is your intuition showing you, leading you and guiding you to the truth.

It's always right.

And it's always there for you.

Start using it every day.

Instead of thinking your way, feel your way on your path.

Feel your intuition and have faith in yourself to listen to it.

It will not steer you wrong.

Day 305

What are you choosing today in your life?

Things you want or things you don't want?

If you are focussing on things you don't want, then you are choosing that.

If you are focussing on things you do want, then you are choosing that.

You can't choose both.

If you are looking at what you don't have, then you are
choosing to have a path that is lacking something.

You will receive more of what you don't have on your path.

You will always be poor, searching for more, lacking,
frustrated, sad, worried, and wondering why.

If you are choosing to see what you have, then
you are choosing a path of abundance.

You will be rich, happy, content, full of love, and living an abundant life.

Start choosing from a place of abundance.

Feel like you are rich, abundant, satisfied, and loving your life and path.

Appreciation, joy, happiness, peace, all these feelings will help
you feel rich and abundant and full of love, and that will
bring everything into your life that you need and want.

Feeling dissatisfied, frustrated for wanting more and not
receiving it, unloving, ungrateful, and unappreciative
will always give you more of that in your life.

Choose your thoughts and words carefully.

They can shift and change who you are and where you are going.

Change who you are.

Choose who you are.

Day 306

You are enough.

You don't need to be different or better or perfect.

You are beautiful inside and out.

Let that shine; let that glow; let it be bright.

You are amazing and magnificent.

You are you, and that's enough.

This message is true, and this message is for you.

Day 307

If you don't heal by doing the inner work involved of letting go of your toxic traits, then nothing in your life will change.

You can move, change jobs, change partners, and let go of people, but everything will still be the same, just in a different spot and with different people.

You will still be toxic.

You will continue to attract the same situations and type of people into your life because you attract who you are from the energy and vibration that you emit into the universe.

You need to learn, grow, change, and evolve in order for your life to truly change.

Learn the lesson from each situation and person.

Forgive and love people, discover the truth about each circumstance, and then let them go.

You can take these lessons you learned so you have more awareness, more knowledge, more compassion, and more love to give to your next path.

If you don't heal, you'll repeat patterns over and over again until you break free of the cycle of karma.

You need to get off the merry-go-round of patterns and move toward healthy ones that serve your higher self.

Learn new things.

Look deep within and find your self-worth and self-respect, knowing that all you need is inside of you.

Know it; feel it; live it; love it; become it and create it.

The Path to Peace

Wouldn't you love to be here, walking through the woods,
taking in the quiet, the peace, the calmness, and the serenity?

To get away from the business of life, to take a
break, and to lose the world for a few hours.

This is where I am every day, being one with nature and God.

This is a little piece of heaven on earth.

Remember to take a break and listen to the nature around you.

It's Time to Believe in Yourself — 381

Day **308**

Living in alignment with the truth is beautiful.

Living in alignment is walking a path of unconditional love for God, for yourself, for your passions, your purpose, and for others.

This is living in the truth of life.

You have to shed your ego, your false self, the lie that you believe is you.

You are only love and that is the path to live on.

The path of love.

Your ego shows you the path of fear and hate.

But it is also here to teach you what love feels like.

Because without fear, you couldn't feel yourself by seeing the opposite of who you are.

When you feel negative emotions, the ego is showing you who you are not.

When you feel who you truly are, you feel positive emotions of love, which feels so good because that is in alignment with who you truly are.

So, if you are leading a life egoistically, you are stressed, disconnected, lacking, sad, lonely, fearful, depressed, angry, anxious, and list goes on and on.

But if you are leading a life of the truth, out of love, your life will be beautiful.

You will have everything you need, and you will feel loved, happy, joyful, excited, abundant, healthy, glowing, and that list can go on and on too.

This is what loving yourself, God, your path, and your life does for you.

Living in alignment with God, the truth, love, changes
your life, your path, and how you see the world and the
illusions in life that you and others have created.

So many people are living a life that is their false self
and not awakening to their true self because they
believe what their egoic mind is telling them.

Walk in the path of the truth and awaken to your
true self and the truth of the universe.

Day 309

Let each step you take be toward the love that is in your life.

Each step is toward transformation and a new you.

Make everything you do be a focus of your
personal growth and your higher self.

Your higher self wants you beside them.

They love you so much.

They are calling you toward them, so you can be
holding hands on your path moving forward.

You are always together in energy, but now you can
feel your higher self, pulling you closer.

With every step you take today, make it be for
you, for your higher good on your path.

That's taking the high road today.

That means choosing yourself first.

If any choice or step goes against your truths, your love, your
higher purpose, or your higher path, don't choose it.

Take the steps that feel good and that are aligned with
your higher purpose, path, and higher self.

Take the steps of love on your path today.

They are taking you to heaven on earth.

Day 310

When you don't take time in your day to rest, recharge, reboot,
and replenish, you can become toxic, sick, and unhealthy.

You need to do something you love in your day that is for you.

You may have a busy life, but it's time to re-evaluate it
and start to say no to things that are not aligned with
your happiness or put them off for other days.

You have to slow down because being busy all the time is not healthy.

Schedule something for you into every day.

Thirty minutes or so can change your life.

You can meditate, go for a walk, listen to a self-help video,
mentor, or music, find a hobby, work on a new skill, write,
craft a passion, or do anything you enjoy that is for you.

It helps to replenish you.

If you don't start taking care of your body, mind, and soul, then
there will be something manifested on your path to stop you or
to slow you down, such as an illness, injury, sickness, or disease.

These are signs that you need to pay attention to.

Take care of yourself and your well-being.

It's your turn.

Your turn should be every day.

You deserve at least thirty minutes for
yourself, to do something you love.

If your life is so busy that you have no time for you, then
it's time to change, slow down, and enjoy your life.

You deserve it.

$\mathcal{D}ay$ 311

Negative emotions are always telling you something
that you need to change inside of you.

Something that you need to heal.

When you have anger for example, it is a trigger.

If you react instead of responding, it's a trigger, and you need to start
asking yourself why you are being triggered by this person or situation.

How can I look at this situation in a different way?

How can I show love in this situation?

What is this situation showing be about myself here in this moment?

Feel your emotions, but also be aware of why you are
hurting or angry or sad so that you will move through them
easier and understand what they are showing you.

You have emotions so that you can see where to heal
and feel love in another person or situation.

It takes time to see these triggers and there are many
layers of healing, but as you practice this awareness you
won't hurt as deep or be triggered because you will see
the why and how and let go and forgive easier.

It won't be as painful over time because of your
new awareness of your emotions.

You will become a happier person when you
are aware of why they are showing up.

Getting to the root of your emotions is healing every time.

Negative emotions can be toxic if you allow them to control you.

For people with mental disorders, depression, addictions,
etc., these negative emotions are toxic.

They suffer deeply because of their negative emotions, becoming toxic to themselves and to the people around them.

Having awareness of your negative emotions and knowing how to heal them and get to the root of them is so important.

Then when they arise, it helps them from growing into bigger problems on your path.

Healing and seeing them for what they are instead of ignoring and stuffing them inside and becoming a toxic person.

Feel them, sit with them, find the cause, then send love to yourself so that you can heal and let them go.

This will heal your triggers and change your life.

Day 312

When we give to others, we receive the love of God
back in return; that is how we are rewarded.

It makes us feel good, especially when we feel
that love of God flowing back into us.

It fills us up again.

We are replenished.

You have the love of God and yourself inside of you to give;
you are always full when you love yourself and God.

Because you are always full of love, you are open to
feeling that love that fills your heart again.

Give with no expectation from others.

Give from a place of love, not for something
in return from another person.

You are blocking this love from God by having an expectation that the
person you are giving your energy to should also be doing the same.

You are disappointed, upset, hurt, and mad that
you have received nothing in return.

But you forget that you are receiving God's love
in return, not love from the other person.

Give with no expectations, out of love for one another, to feel
love and happiness, and out of the goodness of your heart.

You will be replenished and refilled by God's love and
abundance, and you will be blessed on your path from giving
from your heart and with no expectations from others.

That is your gift today for giving from your heart.

Day 313

We are all beautiful flowers in the eyes of God.

We are individually beautiful, no matter what we look like.

We are flowers with different colours.

We are on different paths, but we all need
the same things to grow and be.

We are all flowers, no matter what anyone else has labelled us.

There are no weeds in this world.

We are all flowers, just in different spaces and places, and we
all need the same love and attention to grow and flourish.

Let's stop picking the weeds out because they are flowers too;
we just gave them a label so we can feel better than them.

Flowers and weeds are equally the same.

They grow and flourish the same, when given the same chances.

Flowers are like us.

Made from God, with love, to flourish, show
beauty, and to make others feel love too.

Day 314

Affirm this today:

Today and every day I have faith in myself and on my path
that whatever is meant for me will come for me.

I never have to doubt that faith because God
always has faith in me and my path.

Faith is here for us to feel every day.

I am now in alignment with the faith and love
of God that flows to me every day.

That faith is giving me courage, bravery, patience, and trust that
all I need is on the path that I am stepping toward every day.

I am aligned with that faith.

God can show me the way.

I surrender and have faith in God and myself
today and every day moving forward.

Day 315

You have to live in the moment and let life come to you.

Not try to make things the way you want them to be.

Life doesn't work that way.

You step onto your path in life, and then you choose.

You take another step into life on your path, and then you choose.

Don't worry about life; you can't see what's coming next,
but you can choose each moment when it flows to you.

You don't have to feel lost; you just have to trust that whatever
is coming, you can choose how to handle it when it arises.

If your mind is cluttered with untrue worries, doubts,
and fears, you will always feel anxious and lost.

You will block the clarity with fear and doubt.

You can't live in the present moment when you are
always worried about the future that is really never
here because it is always the present moment.

The now is always here, and every moment is the now.

When you worry about what's going to happen next, you don't
enjoy the present moment, where you are actually living your life.

You have gotten this far and survived.

But stop surviving, and start living.

Love your life now.

Let go of worry; it is useless.

It only adds unnecessary stress to situations.

Worry just adds negative things to your life;
it never makes anything better.

Stop worrying; it's keeping you from enjoying
your life and from living in the now.

Living in the now is where life truly is.

There is no other time; the past is gone, and
the future is always in the now.

Day 316

Today choose yourself.

Today choose to love yourself, who you are, and where you are going.

Today choose to be the best version of you that you can be.

Today choose to believe in God and miracles, and
trust that your life will be amazing because you are
being guided and loved unconditionally.

Today choose to let go of toxic people and situations in
your life so that you can be at peace and happy.

Today start your day by appreciating all that you
are and all that you have in your life.

The time is now to choose a better path, a
better life, and a better mindset.

Today is for you.

Today is the start of a new life for you.

Let that new life and path in, by choosing you first and
letting go of what doesn't serve you anymore.

Today is for you and God.

Day 317

Everything you go through in life is not to bring you down.

Everything you go through in life is to make you stronger.

Everything that happens, happens for a reason.

Everything that is happening is happening to change your life, to help you grow mentally and spiritually, and to teach you life's lessons.

So, when you are in a negative situation, ask yourself:

What am I learning here?

What is there for me to see and to be aware of?

What do I need to change in myself in order
to see this situation differently?

What is this person showing me here?

Look at the situation as an opportunity rather than a challenge.

A new perspective will change everything.

Day 318

The light is always there.

Always.

You have to keep choosing to see it.

When you turn away from the light, you are turning away from the love that God is giving you every minute of every day of your life.

God is with you, beside you, and in you.

God is everywhere that you are.

God doesn't go into the darkness, though.

You have to go to God into the light that is shining so bright for you right now.

When you love yourself the way God loves you, you will feel it so deeply.

Stop listening to that negative voice inside your head.

That's not God's voice.

That's your ego's voice.

And it wants to keep you away from that love of God because it isn't even aware of God.

Turn to that light of God and hear the soft, encouraging, uplifting voice that will guide you to a new, unconditional loving path.

God is in you; you are God; God is you.

Day 319

We are all unique, and we are all special.

We are all here for the same things, but we
are doing them in individual ways.

We all have our own gifts, talents, and passions that
we develop for certain paths in this lifetime.

If we keep looking at what others have, we will miss
out on what we have to offer the world.

All of our souls are on the same journey but with
different purposes to fulfill on our own paths.

We come to this planet to experience being human and to
experience it in a way that only we as individuals can know.

We come to create a life of joy, happiness, peace, and abundance, with
faith and trust that we will have all of that and more on our paths.

We also come to this earth to learn, to grow, and to evolve our souls
in this lifetime, and that's our own unique journey on the way.

Our souls, our angels, our guides, our spirits, and God know the
path to this, and they are lighting that path for each of us.

We are all individually divine, connected, one, and have our own
gifts, talents, and passions that we share with everyone we meet.

We are all souls, creating the best path and
life that we can love and enjoy.

We are all about creation, love, peace, happiness, abundance,
appreciation, and trusting the universe and God on our way.

Day 320

Changing your vibration to a positive one can be done by focussing on the positive, the good, being happy, and changing your mindset.

Stop blaming people for your emotions, let go of the past, heal your wounds, and stop worrying.

Meditate, walk and spend time in nature, connect with God, and pray for guidance, support, and help.

All of these things and more change your energy and vibration.

Start focussing on yourself, on your internal world, your inner peace, and your inner happiness.

Day 321

Change is a good thing if you understand why it is happening.

You can't stay the same.

You are here to create, grow, evolve, expand your mind, and experience and love life and yourself unconditionally.

Change is showing you these things.

You cannot stop it.

Let change happen and let an amazing new path come into your life.

Stop resisting it and start embracing it.

Day 322

Your vibration and energy show you everything.

You are vibration and energy; all of us are.

We are all vibrating at different frequencies and consciousness.

If you are living in a low vibration, then you will feel frustrated, angry, depressed, sad, hurt, dwell on the past, fear life and the future, have low self-esteem, low self-worth, no boundaries, blame others for your problems, have no respect for yourself, and look for others to love you and make you happy.

If you are living in a high vibration, you will feel happiness, love, joy, peace, calmness, self-worth, self-respect, abundant, appreciation, gratitude, ease and flow, live in the moment, not blame others for your problems, have healthy boundaries, have self- awareness, no anxiety, and have self-love and self- care.

You will be free, healthy and vibrant, beautiful on the inside and out, and glowing and smiling with unconditional love for you and others.

If you are in a negative vibration, this will manifest more negative people, situations, drama, toxicity, etc., into your life.

If you are in a positive vibration, you will attract more of that into your life.

You will attract perfect situations and people you need who are like you, and more of everything positive that you are asking for will manifest into your path and life.

Soul mates, money, good jobs and opportunities, balance, peace, support, and love.

At the positive vibration of energy, your life will be in alignment with who you truly are, and you will have guidance that you can hear from your higher self.

It is so important to keep a positive mindset and vibration to get the things you want in your life.

God wants you to have everything you ask for.

Being negative stops that, reflecting what you are vibrating and giving you more of it.

Start cleaning up your vibration so that you can be the best version of yourself you can be you.

You can be who you truly are in this lifetime.

Day 333

It's always an effort when you are not following your excitement.

When you follow your excitement, you will do amazing things.

This is your inspiration, and your mind transcends
and opens up to everything you are wanting.

Things come alive in your mind when you are excited.

Your soul is speaking to you when you are having fun.

This is who you are.

You are made of excitement, happiness, and bliss.

Keep following that path; it's going to amazing places.

Day 334

What you are creating is from your own mind.

What you are focussing on, you're creating.

And getting more of it as it goes.

If you are focussing on the bad, you will see the bad all around you.

If you are focussing on the good, you will see the good all around you.

Your thoughts and focus are the most important things you can change.

When you change our thoughts, your whole life
shifts and changes to the new focus.

Look around you today.

What do you see in your life?

What life are you creating today?

Day 335

Acceptance of the moment for what is, is how to live in the moment.

Acceptance.

You can't change it or control it.

So, you have to accept what it is and know that
this moment is here for you, for a reason.

A reason to see more clearly, and a reason to
make better choices than before.

This moment is showing you something
inside of you if you are judging it.

It's showing you where you need to heal in that moment and see
the love for you, another, the situation, and the world around you.

Each moment is for you to see beauty, love, God, and your true self.

If it is reflecting something other than that, then you
need to see it more clearly and ask yourself why you are
judging or not liking this moment for what it is?

There is no changing the moment, only the way you look at it.

A positive mindset and perspective can help you
see the moment for what it truly is.

Accept the moment.

Love the moment.

Live in the moment.

Be the moment.

It's for you and your experience only.

Day 336

You have to start caring about your own well-being and your love for yourself.

Do you really love and care about yourself?

It's not about what others think about you.

It's about what you think about you.

Your life is about you: your well-being, your healing, and your love for yourself.

It's not about what others think and comparing them to you.

Stop looking to others to love and care for you and for their approval.

You have to love and care for yourself first.

Going within for the love of God as well.

The love that you have for yourself, and God are the only relationships that truly matter.

When you look elsewhere for love, you are not feeling your own love or God's love.

You are missing out on it when you are seeking it from outside of yourself.

It's not out there.

It's in you, and it's in God.

You are not aligned with the unconditional love that you both have when you are looking outside of your own energy and vibration.

Those people you are seeking it from have to do the same.

They cannot love you first, then themselves.

And you cannot love them first, then yourself.

It doesn't work that way.

The truth to happiness and being in love with your
life and your path is loving who you are deeply inside,
the way you are loved unconditionally by God.

Love yourself like that.

Feel that deep love flowing to you.

Everyone needs to do this, then they can love everyone with
that same love and happiness and peace that is now in them.

That love fills you up and fills your heart, and it
will overflow to the others around you.

Feel that feeling before seeking it from others.

You will just get emptiness and conditional love from
them if they are not deeply loving themselves

as well.

Love is within, and it changes your life and who you are.

God's love, your love, and the universe's
love will fill you up and heal you.

You are loved so deeply.

Start knowing this and filling yourself up with that deep, unconditional
love that wraps around you and surrounds you every day.

Day 337

You are amazing; you are beautiful; you are loved unconditionally.

God loves us all equally every minute of our life.

God know what your true self looks and feels like.

God know what you need to live and love your life unconditionally.

God is giving you all that you need today and every day.

It's all around you.

Your life will be amazing if you see the true
beauty inside of you and in the universe.

Love yourself so you can wake up to a new perspective
and a new way of seeing the world you live in.

See yourself through the eyes of God.

It's a beautiful view that only you and God can see from your eyes.

Day 338

Affirm this:

I am living my truest self today.

My soul, my body, and my mind are in
alignment with my path and my life.

My soul is leading my path and my journey, and I am following the
path of passion, love, peace, excitement, ease and flow, beauty and bliss.

My truest self feels like heaven.

I don't live for anyone else but me.

This might sound selfish, but it isn't.

This is how we are supposed to live.

In true happiness, true love, true peace, and in true joy.

My soul will lead me to my true passions, gifts, and
talents, which I will use to help others and to give
more and more when I live to be my truest self.

I am in alignment, and my soul will lead
me to the most beautiful paths.

That will help me to create a beautiful life
of love, peace, joy, and happiness.

I will start following my passions, the ones that make
my heart sing and soar because that's where my life
will start to change into something amazing.

That's my truest self and my truest essence.

I am truly one on this path with my soul.

The Lotus Flower

This flower represents, purity, rebirth, and strength.

All of which we need on our path to grow and transform into something more magnificent than we can even imagine.

The lotus flower for me is the light inside of us that comes out of the darkness and changes us into beauty.

It grows in the mud and in the darkness and transforms into a beautiful flower.

This is spirituality, and it speaks to me.

We transform from the darkness.

We grow.

Day 339

What you are seeing in toxic people is a reflection of yourself as well.

If you are triggered by someone or something, it means
you have something that also needs healing in you.

Toxic people also show you the toxic parts
of you that you need to let go of.

Be aware of them.

See them and heal them.

Let them go if you can.

We all have something that we think we have dealt with and healed
from, but then sometimes something on a deeper level shows up.

If you are triggered by something, it always means there is
something more that a person or situation is showing you.

If you are truly healed and have let go and forgiven the other
person and yourself, then you will respond, not react.

Your triggers will no longer control you.

You will have control now.

You will have the power now to move forward
without the toxicity in you.

You are free.

You are at peace.

$\mathcal{D}ay$ **340**

In this moment we are thinking, moving, breathing, seeing, watching, hearing, smelling, touching, observing, analyzing, reflecting, tasting,

and feeling.

We are doing all of this in unawareness.

If we stopped and slowed down to appreciate all of these things in this moment, we would be enjoying the present moment.

We would be in awareness instead of unawareness in life.

If we stopped to savour the moment, we would enjoy our life so much more.

We would see the beauty all around us that the earth and the universe has created for us.

It is for us to enjoy.

It truly was made for us.

If you slowed down your life, you would appreciate the flowers, the birds, the trees, your food, your children, your spouse, your parents, your life, your job, and so much more.

Choosing to slow down your life and be still more often in your body and mind will help you connect with your soul, the earth, your soul tribe, your path, your journey, and with God.

Slow down and watch the birds, smell the flowers, or kiss your children or spouse every day.

It changes your life.

Day 341

You need to truly love yourself unconditionally
and not put yourself down.

Talk to yourself like you are your own best friend.

You should be anyway.

Believe in yourself, and don't doubt yourself.

Most people, especially those with anxiety, depression,
and mental disorders, are listening to that loud
voice in their head, which is their ego.

They are letting their ego run the show, listening
to and following that guidance.

The ego's guidance leads nowhere but to
negativity and toxic behaviours.

It leads to fear, defeat, frustration, hate, anger, low self-esteem,
low self-worth, unhappiness, deflation, and depression.

The ego sets people up for failure every time.

When you stop listening to that voice in your head and start
listening to the intuition that God has built into each of us as
a guidance system, you are led to love, happiness, peace, joy,
calmness, inner peace, inspiration, and real success in our life.

Follow your heart, your intuition, your gut
instinct; it gets you everywhere.

Following your heart is the way to live.

It leads you to more in life.

It leads you to everything you want.

Day 342

Peace is the core of your true self.

Peace is who you are.

To feel peace, love who you are, love what you
are doing, and love where you are going.

To feel peace in your life, let go of your egoic
mind; it only creates chaos and drama.

To feel at peace, sit with your own mind in silence; that's where it is.

Peace is the way of life, the way to happiness,
and the way to who you really are.

Day 343

Your spirit leads you everywhere.

Everything that feels good, your spirit has led you there.

Your spirit knows everything you want.

You have so many spirit guides, angels, God,
guiding you to everything that is for you.

It's a beautiful dance when you start to listen to the
song that they are singing to you in your ears.

Your spirit dances with you every day.

It has the lead, even though you think you do.

Spirit is dancing, and you are its partner for eternity.

Let the spirit flow with you, around you, through you, and for you.

It's a beautiful dance on the path to life.

Day 344

Depending on someone else such as a partner to
make you happy is call co-dependency.

This is being dependent on someone else to bring you happiness.

In this process you are also trying to please your partner
so that they will not be angry at you or reject you for your
actions; you lose yourself in this type of relationship.

They are not responsible for your happiness.

You are responsible for you in every way.

You are responsible for your own happiness, freedom,
peace, joy, love, well-being, and independence.

Nothing outside of you can do this for you.

This is why you feel empty, alone, and sad, because you
are depending on others or material things to fill you
up with what you are not doing for yourself.

They are responsible for their own path,
happiness, energy, and vibration.

You try to change others to suit your own personal needs on your path.

This is unhealthy.

Change your own way to help your own self on your own path.

Be responsible for you, your thoughts, your actions, and
your emotions; they are no one else's but your own.

This is how healthy people, relationships,
and paths are formed and built.

This is how you end toxic relationships, by stopping
the dependency of others in your life.

You come together as healed people full of love for yourself, and you then co-create a life together as whole partners.

This will end co-dependency, and you can have a beautiful, lasting relationship with another.

Heal yourself.

Love yourself.

Become a healthy person for you, not for anyone else.

You are worth it.

Don't be co-dependent.

Be independent.

$\mathcal{D}ay$ 345

Every day you need to work on yourself.

Every day you need to help yourself to be a
better person than you were yesterday.

Be aware of your consciousness on your path, as it helps
you become aware of your thoughts, emotions, words,
mindset, and your feelings toward others and yourself.

You are never done doing this work, and when you do this
consciously, you change who you are deliberately.

You deliberately choose to make your life better
instead of unconsciously walking your path and
hurting others and yourself on the way.

Awareness is what you should be looking to achieve every day.

Looking through the eyes of awareness helps you to let go
of the illusions that the subconscious is bringing to you.

Your subconscious is blind and when you live in that
unawareness, you create in the dark and in fear.

Awareness from your consciousness brings
light and love to your life and path.

You see the truth, and then you can make better
choices on your path from this awareness.

This is who you truly are meant to be.

When you see your life through awareness, it changes your
perspective, your choices, your feelings, your emotions,
and you have more clarity in this new light of love.

Awareness is your true self show you the way and the
path to a new way of being, seeing, and living.

Be aware on your path; it changes who you are.

Day 346

We are all spiritual beings in this universe.

This is not a religion.

It is who we are.

We are not human beings; we are spirits.

We are souls.

We are having a human experience in this moment.

We have so much inside of us that we haven't even discovered yet.

We are extensions of God's energy.

We are souls connected to the universe by our energy and vibration.

When we start to know this truth, we will begin to
understand who we truly are and why we are here.

We are made in the eyes of God, the universe, the
creator, source energy, whatever we call God.

There is only one God, which is pure positive
energy and unconditional love.

God is energy is our energy as well, as we are made from God's energy.

God's energy is the frequency of unconditional love.

That's God's energy, and that's our energy.

Our souls are connected with God's energy.

Therefore, we are one and the same; we are
all connected as one by our souls.

Everything in this universe is, as it is all made by God with his energy.

We are all spiritual.

We are all connected with each other, with animals, nature, space, planets, star, the sun, the spirit realm, etc.,

We are all one.

We are all powerful creators.

Once we discover this, we awaken to a new way of seeing the world around us.

We see love, the light of God, and the light in us.

We awaken to the truth, and it's truly beautiful.

Day 347

True beauty needs no mask.

True beauty is alignment of who you truly are.

Loving yourself authentically and unconditionally for
who you are and for the path that you are on.

True beauty only sees love and compassion.

True beauty is inside of each and every one of us.

Let it out for the world to see.

Drop all the masks and live in pure unconditional love for yourself.

Love yourself so much that it overflows to others.

Love yourself so much that you will shine and glow inside and out.

Love yourself every day so that you can see the true
beauty that is in each and every soul, you included.

Your mask is dimming your light.

Take it off, and shine bright.

Day 348

Everyone needs to be uplifted and encouraged.

Everyone needs to be complimented instead of criticized.

Are you someone who criticizes or compliments?

What does criticizing do to a person.

It makes them feel bad, down, like a failure,
less than enough, and like quitting.

What does a compliment do for a person?

It makes them feel good, better, whole, proud, happy,
full, like they are enough, let's them keep going, and
helps them to improve more and more.

Next time you have something to say to someone, think of
how you are going to make them feel with your words.

These will probably stay with them.

Your words could make or break them.

Stop.

Think first.

Speak kindly always.

Make a person's day better.

It's important.

It's simple and easy to be kind.

$\mathcal{Day}$ 349

Affirm this:

Thank you, angels, guides, God, and my spiritual team.

I am truly blessed every day with the guidance, help,
and inspiration that I receive from you.

You are with me through thick and thin.

You are with me when I may forget that you are with me.

You never forget me or leave me.

You are with me when I have lost my way, and
you always bring me back on track.

You are with me when I have lost my faith in
myself, and you always have faith in me.

You always have the answer I need when I am searching for one.

I am truly blessed to have such support, guidance, and help on my path.

My team is amazing and know me so well.

Thank you for being with me today and every day to show me the
way to my purpose, my path, my passions, and all that I love.

I love you all so much unconditionally, and I
know I am loved back with enormously.

It's a beautiful feeling to know I am never alone and never will be.

It's a beautiful feeling to know that love is with me every day.

Thank you for being by my side.

I ask you to help me today, to guide me today,
and to show me the way today.

You are appreciated by me so much today and every day.

Day 350

We are all light.

The darkness is leaving to make room for more light.

It's growing inside every one of us right now.

It is the lightest it has ever been within us,
now and forever, moving forward.

We are all energy of light, and we are all shining bright today.

We are receiving this beautiful light from God, the
creator, to transform us into who we truly are.

We are of a higher consciousness and awareness that
is coming to us from this beautiful light.

So, step into this light and let go of the darkness
you are carrying within you.

It doesn't serve you anymore.

It doesn't belong with you anymore.

The darkness cannot survive with all the
light that is surrounding you now.

You are light, and it is the way to the new
world you are stepping into now.

Shed the dark, the bad habits, the old ways, and
the old you; it's time for it to all go.

It's time for you now to step into the light of God
that is waiting for you to feel and see and be.

The time is now to become the light you were always meant to be.

Day 351

We are always forgiven by God.

God always loves us unconditionally.

When we align with our strengths, we are
aligning with the energy of God.

We have to have faith in ourself as well, just as God does in us.

We have to do the work that we are inspired to do by God.

He gives us that strength and helps us to feel our own
love inside; he gives us love and inspires us to feel
his unconditional love that is always there.

So, have faith and belief in yourself, and you will have
the strength and courage to keep moving forward.

God gives that to you, and you have to align
with it to feel it inside of yourself.

God has the power, but so do you.

Don't give up on yourself because God never gives up on you.

God is always by your side, loving you unconditionally.

He is in you, and you are God, and you create your life with God.

His love and faith are flowing to you always.

Feel it, and know it, and step into it.

You are loved, and you are blessed, and you are one.

Day 352

Suffering ends when you choose to end it.

Suffering ends when you stop looking at the
bad and start looking at the good.

Suffering ends when you know things happen for a reason in your life.

Suffering ends when you live from a place of love and
see it all around you, within you, and in others.

Suffering ends when you know you are here to create, not to suffer.

Suffering ends when you see the light of the universe.

Suffering is a choice of your mindset.

Suffering is lacking love inside of you.

Suffering is showing you love.

Without suffering, you cannot see love on your path.

God didn't put you here to suffer.

He put you here to create and to be love.

See love, the higher power, the higher path and
purpose, the light of love, the good, and God in your
life, and the suffering will fade and fall away.

Suffering is a choice.

Choose love instead, and change your path and yourself.

Day 353

Everything in your life happens for a reason.

There are no coincidences on your path.

When something bad happens, it's here to teach you something.

It's teaching you lessons in life, like it's time to change, for soul growth, to improve, to evolve, to heal, to love more, to love yourself more, to remove toxic people and or toxic habits from your life, to let go, to surrender to God, to become more positive, to be happier, and to appreciate what you have.

There are so many reasons to see things more clearly in your life and on your path.

So, don't let life get you down.

See the reasons, the gifts, the lessons in every situation, circumstance, and person that comes to you.

God put them there, and you attracted them to help you along your way on your path.

Instead of asking why is this happening to you, ask what it is teaching you so that you can improve your life and change for the better.

The less you resist, the faster the new situation will come to you.

Let go of hurting and suffering, and learn from the situation.

You don't need to continue to suffer; you need to change, grow, and evolve into something beautiful and amazing.

It's waiting for you, but you have to be in a place of letting go of the suffering before it will come to you.

Suffering blocks your path and slows everything down.

Learning speeds up the growth on your path,
allowing you to flourish once again.

Learn, grow, evolve, and create something better and new.

That's what you are truly here for today and every day.

Day 354

Embrace the light side of things.

If you embrace the dark side, you are honouring your ego.

You are bringing it forward.

You are affirming that you love the dark side,
which is weakness, and your small mind.

You are making it stronger.

If you embrace the light side, your strengths, and positive traits
and attributes, then they will take you out of the darkness.

Embracing and honouring the dark only adds fuel to it.

Embracing the light gives way for more light so
that the darkness can no longer live.

You have to embrace your courage, bravery, strength, and love.

Not your sadness, not your fears, and not your shame.

These are your weaknesses that are illusions given to you by your ego.

You feed them more when you embrace them.

See why your weaknesses are in your life and
look at them for what they are.

Ask how you can change these into a positive
vibration instead of honouring the negative vibration
that takes you deeper into the darkness.

Learn the lessons from the dark side, and let go of the rest.

Show love that you learned something new about
life, and grow from any dark experiences.

That's what they are there for; to show you who you are
not and to let you embrace who you truly are.

You are not dark; you are light.

You need to embrace the strengths that took you out of the darkness.

Honour your light.

That is your true self; darkness is your false self.

You want to live in the truth, not fear, so embrace
your strengths to get out of the darkness.

Day 355

Today just live your life and make better choices.

Be happy.

Show love.

Let things go.

See the reason and the lesson.

See the beauty all around you and in you.

That's what you are here for every day.

To enjoy every moment of the day.

Being thankful, appreciative, and grateful for everything you have and for everything that happens.

Love your life today.

Day 356

What a beautiful day to be you.

What a great time to live your best life today.

Smile and breath and walk the path that is meant for you.

It is unfolding with every step you take.

Your love is flowing everywhere you go today and every day.

Do you feel it flowing and swirling all around you like the wind?

Be full of love so you can help others on their path today.

You need to feel that warm, bright, light energy that
is growing within you and on your path.

Your love lights up others and you, today and every day.

Smile and breath and keep walking the
path that is meant for you today.

Show your love on your path as you go.

It's meant to be free to flow to those who need it.

Your love is for you to share.

It overflows in you when you walk the path that is meant for you.

$\mathcal{D}$ay 357

To anyone giving so many chances to others in
their life, you need to learn from this them.

You both do.

You are both learning lessons from each other.

That is why this person or situation keeps coming
back to you over and over again.

Learn, grow, evolve, and change.

That is what each situation brings you every time.

Stop letting this merry-go-round keep going around and around.

You have to get off by learning from it.

Then you can keep moving forward with or without the other person.

If they didn't learn, let them go a different way with someone else.

You can continue to live on a new path, moving forward,
but off the merry-go-round that was keeping you stuck.

You need to learn from every situation and from
every person you meet and encounter.

That's the reason for being here.

To learn and evolve.

Stop being stuck in your life.

Learn from it.

If something keeps repeating for you, this is why.

Life is always teaching you to change your behaviour, to shed your old ways that don't work, to stop living in your ego, and to let go of toxic patterns and people that are stopping you from growing and moving forward.

Are you learning on your path, or are you still on the merry-go-round, not knowing how to get off?

Day 358

This moment is more precious than you think.

This moment is where you choose your life from.

You choose where you go, what to do, who to do it with, and you decide your life from this very moment, every moment.

This is where your life is.

Right now.

You can change your life in any moment.

You have to choose it.

You have to choose to be present in the moment to experience how the moment feels for you.

If you are distracted by past hurts in this moment, you will feel that past energy instead of the now energy.

You bring that hurt energy to the now as if you are still living there.

This is why the present moment is more important than you think.

If you are worried and in fear of the future, then you will bring that fear to the now moment.

Are you being present in the moment to experience the true feeling of love that is happening in the now?

Or are you are making decisions based off the past and future energy in the now moment?

That's why this moment, the present, the now, is so precious, more than you even know.

Start living in the now, so you can choose your life with the true feelings of the present.

That's why this moment is so precious.

Be present in the now, and your life will change for the better.

Day 359

I am the light for you.

If you are my friend, I am shining it brightly for you always.

My hand is always out for you to hold and
to guide you out of the darkness.

Stand in my light, my friend, and I will shine.

My light doesn't dim in the dark; it shines brighter for you.

My light is for you, my friend.

Please take my hand, and I will guide you out.

I will show you your own light now to shine on your path.

You are bright; you are light; let it shine now.

Your path is lighting up now that you are out of the
darkness of the ego and in the light and love of God.

Keep going; you are the light of your life.

Day 360

Affirm this:

Today I reflect back on my path for a moment
to see how far I have come this year.

I have grown so much, and I have changed my life for the better.

I am becoming the soul I want to be.

Aligned with my truth and my true self.

I reflect back on my path to see that my light is brighter today.

I am proud of the work I have done to become this person I am today.

My heart space has become wide open, and
I live my life from this space.

It's leading the way now.

I have mastered my life today as I look back
and see how far I have come.

I am living a life of love, happiness, peace, faith, joy, and so much more.

This is an authentic and true path that I am living.

I am led by God, my soul, my guides, and they
have led me to this beautiful path I am on.

As I reflect on my path, I know I have gained so much knowledge
and wisdom, and I am proud of who I have become.

It doesn't take much time to become a new person.

It does take dedication, focus, and faith to change and grow.

I love who I am becoming more and more every day.

I look forward to the new year coming.

Who will I become in the next year, and what is next from me?

What amazing things does God have in store
for me on my path moving forward?

I love the journey.

I can't wait for more on my path.

How exciting it is to see it unfold in front of me, step by step.

I look forward to even more new for me.

Day 361

How can you become more positive when
there is turmoil all around you?

You have to choose it.

You have to choose it in every moment.

To be negative or positive.

They both have the same effort but totally
different effects on your path.

Negativity and positivity play a part in every situation.

Being negative adds more fuel to the fire as
well as more chaos and turmoil.

Then you attract more of it.

Seeing the positive in each situation can free you from that turmoil.

It can change it into a lesson for you, a gift.

There is a positive side in every circumstance,
but you have to choose to see it.

Seeing the positive will take you out of the situation
faster and easier, as more positive energy will flow to you
and through you, bringing solutions to your path.

What are you learning from the situation or person in front of you?

Everything teaches you, and when you see the lesson,
you see the positive and where you need to change
your perspective of what you are experiencing.

This situation may be teaching you to be patient,
to be kind, or to show more love.

Each circumstance is always a reflection of your inner self.

Every situation shows you that you need to change
your perspective, mindset, or vibration.

You attract what you are, so if you are focussing
on the negative that's around you, then that's the
vibration you are sending out in the moment.

If you are seeing the beauty, the love, the gift in the situation,
then you are shifting your vibration to positive and raising your
vibe, and you can now let more positive energy onto your path.

Day 362

Life is a journey.

A journey of discovery.

A journey to become your true self.

Life is about inner love, peace, and happiness and discovering the truth about who you truly are.

You are love.

You are peace.

You are joy.

You are more than you can even imagine.

You are a gift from God, here to discover who you truly are by experiencing who you are not.

You are not like anyone else.

Each person is a gift from God, given beautiful qualities to find inside them.

You are not here to suffer, put others down, or to compare your life to others.

You are not here to hate, judge, hurt, or be the same as anyone else.

This life is a discovery of yourself.

This life is to evolve your soul and to become one with God again.

This journey is about going back home to God and aligning with your creator again, as you once were when you were created.

God loves you deeply and wants you to create a soul and life and path that you love deeply.

You need to feel this deep love for yourself again, discover the truth of who you truly are, then embrace and live it.

This journey is about finding yourself, then
stepping into it and becoming it.

Love is the way to the truth that will set you free.

The truth is about love, loving yourself, and loving who you are.

If you are putting love in someone else's hands,
you will never feel the truth of yourself.

You have to find yourself and the truth of who you truly are.

Love is the way to finding who you truly are.

Love is the answer.

Love you, love your path, love others, love God unconditionally.

Unconditional love changes us, it shows us the way to the truth.

Unconditional love shows us peace, happiness, joy, bliss
and these are the truths of what is inside of us.

If you want the truth, then start to feel the love that
is in you, that love will fill you up, that love will make
you whole again, that love will set you free.

That love is what God wants you to feel, and to be
and to share with all that surrounds you.

Love is the truth and the way.

Love is you.

Love shows you who you truly are.

Day 363

The outside world should not dictate your inner world.

The outside world is falling apart around you.

The outside world is chaos, fear, hate, anger, and so much more.

The outside world should not control your inner world.

Your inner world is full of love, peace, happiness, and joy.

This is the true world.

If we all stopped looking at the outside world for answers to our problems, that outside world would cease to exist for us.

It would change the world.

If we all went within ourself and turned off the outside world, it would have to transform.

We give so much of our attention to the news, politicians, world disasters, and chaos, and what we focus on, we create.

Nothing is outside of us.

We need to take our power back by shutting off the world and going within to our own universe.

Each of us has the power to do this.

We need to choose our own love, peace, and happiness on the inside, then feel it and know it is ours.

Create a new world by choosing peace instead of war and happiness over fear, worry, and doubt.

The power is up to us; we can change the world by seeking answers and finding love from within ourself.

The universe and the power to transform lives is within us.

It will move us forward into a peaceful path.

We need to stop creating a world we don't want and start creating one we do.

$\mathcal{D}ay$ 364

Love fills me up today; it's everywhere.

I don't have to go anywhere to feel it.

I don't have to be anyone to feel it.

I don't have to have anything to feel it.

It's inside of me, flowing through me easily.

I don't have to do anything or be anyone to feel it.

It just flows.

I just have to be to feel it.

I just have to be who I truly am, and love is always there.

No matter where I go, I can feel it.

I don't need anyone to give it to me because
it's already here inside of me.

I am the source of that love.

That love that fills me up comes from within me.

I don't need to seek it from anyone, from anywhere, or from anything.

Love is everywhere, and when I feel it from the inside,
it will fill me up, and it will make me whole.

I am love, and I am the source of love.

If I find that love that's within me to fill myself up,
I don't need to look any further than that.

Day 365

Today you are home again.

Today you stepped into the light of God fully.

Today you are together with God again.

Aligned in the light of his pure, unconditional love.

It was always there; that energy never leaves.

God has been with each of us from the beginning.

He lets us lead on our path.

God lets us learn and grow as he watches his children evolve, change, and experience our life in this universe and on this earth.

God lets us be free to choose which way to go.

He lets us lead, and God enjoys the ride no matter where we go.

We are divinely protected on the way.

We can ask for direction, and he will show us the way.

God is always showing us the way back home to him.

We have the choice to make it whatever path we desire.

Some of us take longer, enjoying the adventure;
some learn quickly, then come back for more.

We learn as we go and as we find our way
back home to the light of God.

We can get into dark places, where we can't see or
feel the light of God our Father anymore.

We need to call out for help, and God will pull us out.

He will put us back on the path home.

God is always watching all of us, his children, and loving us as we go.

God is creating and experiencing with us every step of the way.

We can get so lost in the dark that we cannot hear, feel,
or see that love of God that is always there for us.

So, ask for help; your Father is always there.

Find that love and light purely and truly again.

Align with God's energy and light to shine bright again.

Feel God's love that surrounds you so lovingly.

Today you are home with God.

God has led you back to heaven here on earth.

Feel God's love that is in you too.

You are God, and God is you.

Take his hand and let him lead you back home.

The Journey Never Ends

I hope these words have helped you
change, grow, and evolve.

I hope they have helped you to see a new
way of living, seeing, and being.

I hope these words have helped you step
onto the path of your true self.

I hope they have helped you to believe in yourself and your path again.

This book was made to help you heal, to let go of your past,
and to live in the present moment, where all your life is.

I wrote this book to help you see who God truly is, that you are a
part of that source energy, that you are loved on a higher, deeper level,
and that you are so much more than you can even imagine you are.

We are all light; we are all love; we are all energy; we are all souls; we
are all God, and we are all one with that source energy that created us.

We are all spiritual beings, but we are also way more than that.

We are beautiful, amazing, and loved so deeply by God and by our
spiritual team that surrounds us, protects us, and guides us on our path.

The journey never ends, even after our body dies, because we move
forward into the spiritual realm, growing, learning, changing, and
evolving, moving forward and higher to the path of enlightenment.

Never stop loving yourself, believing in yourself, or moving forward.

Love yourself, your path, your life, and others unconditionally;
it changes your life and the ones around you.

Heal, love, and be true to you.

You are the only one who matters in your life, so put yourself and God first, then you can create beautiful, healthy relationships and raise your family from a better place of knowledge and wisdom and with unconditional love.

It's time to believe in you.

T. O'Brien

About the Author
Tammy OBrien

Tammy OBrien is a spiritual life coach and mentor, that helps many people believe in themselves. She is a spiritually awakened soul with a higher purpose to inspire others on their path.

She helps people to see a new way of looking at their own self, and to help them to heal from there past so that they can move forward into a better life and future.

She shows people why we are here, how the universe works, what God is, and to help you align with the truth of who you really are. She has inspired so many with her online Facebook group **Its Time to Believe in Yourself,** and helped many see the way to new way of living and being.

The true way.

If you are lost and looking to find yourself this book is for you. This will align you with your higher self, your soul and with God on your path.

Visit

www.itstimetobelieveinyourself.com
for one on one coaching and mentoring and start to believe in yourself today.

Printed in the USA
CPSIA information can be obtained
at www.ICGtesting.com
LVHW050200221123
764524LV00039B/1122/J